KEY FACTS

EQUITY AND
TRUSTS

CHRIS TURNER

D0171260

Hodder & Stoughton

A MEMBER OF THE HODDER HEADLINE GROUP

Orders: please contact Bookpoint Ltd, 130 Milton Park, Abingdon, Oxon OX14 4SB.
Telephone: (44) 01235 827720, Fax: (44) 01235 400454. Lines are open 9.00–6.00,
Monday to Saturday, with a 24-hour message answering service.
You can also order through our website: www.hodderheadline.co.uk

British Library Cataloguing in Publication Data
A catalogue record for this title is available from The British Library.

ISBN 0 340 87173 3

First published 2003
Impression number   10 9 8 7 6 5 4 3 2
Year   2007 2006 2005 2004

Copyright © 2002 Chris Turner

Cover design by Stewart Larking
Typeset by Transet Limited, Coventry, England.
Printed in Great Britain for Hodder & Stoughton Educational, a division of Hodder Headline,
338 Euston Road, London NW1 3BH by Cox & Wyman Ltd, Reading, Berkshire.

CONTENTS

PREFACE

The Key Facts series is a practical and complete revision aid that can be used by students of law courses at all levels from A Level to degree and beyond, and in professional and vocational courses. Equity and trusts is generally studied only at degree level or above in either postgraduate or on some professional courses, and also on ILEX Part 2 courses.

The Key Facts series is designed to give a clear view of each subject. This will be useful to students when tackling new topics and is invaluable as a revision aid. Most chapters open with an outline in diagram form of the points covered in that chapter. The points are then developed in a structured list form to make learning easier. Supporting cases are given throughout by name and, for some complex areas, facts are given to reinforce the point being made.

The Key Facts series aims to accommodate the syllabus content of most qualifications in a subject area, using many visual learning aids.

The topics covered for equity and trusts include all of those contained in mainstream syllabuses. Equity and trusts is often seen as a fairly dry and dull area. In fact it is actually more relevant to most people's lives than, for example, criminal law, which is a very popular area of study. Anyone who jointly owns a domestic home or who wants to leave property in a will to underage children, or who has anything to do with charity work or who has a private pension, for instance, would be able to identify what a very practical and useful subject it is.

The law is stated as I believe it to be on 1st December 2002.

CHAPTER 1

INTRODUCTION TO EQUITY AND TRUSTS

History of Equity:	Equitable maxims
• Defects in common law writ system and inadequate remedies • Petitioning of king for fair solution as 'fountain of justice' • Delegation of task to Lord Chancellor • Creation of separate Court of Chancery – staffed by clerics • Solutions based on discretion of court • Conflict in *Earl of Oxford's case* – in conflict, equity prevails • Merged with common law in Judicature Acts 1873 and 1875 • Still developing, eg search orders and freezing injunctions	• Equity acts *in personam* • Equity looks to intention, not the form • Delay defeats equity • Equity regards that which should be done as being done • Equity is equality • He who comes to equity must come with clean hands • Equity will not assist a volunteer • First in time prevails • Equity will not suffer a wrong to be without a remedy • Equity will not allow statute to be used as an engine of fraud • Equity follows the law
Equitable remedies	**Definition/classification of trusts**
• injunctions – to prevent occurrences such as a breach of trust • specific performance – to ensure a contract is carried out • rescission – to return parties to a pre-contractual position • rectification – to change a document to reflect an actual agreement	• settlor/donor transfers real or personal property to trustee to use for benefit of beneficiaries or for purposes (charity) • can be expressed by settlor, implied by law or statutory • can be private (human beneficiaries) or public, eg charitable purposes • can be fixed (settlor's terms) or discretionary (decided by trustee)
Equitable interests	**Context of Trusts**
• mortgage – to allow larger loans with security for lender, based on legal title • lien – to hold property till a debt paid • restrictive covenants – to retain control over use of land sold • easements – to enable legitimate use of another person's land • the trust itself – a means of splitting legal and beneficial ownership to protect beneficial owner by allowing him to enforce terms of trust	• pension funds • investment – unit trusts • security for loans • voluntary arrangements with creditors • NHS trusts • trade union funds • co-ownership • clubs and unincorporated associations • charities • non-charitable purposes • protection of minors • nominees in property transfers • protective trusts • secret trusts • preserving wealth • disputes over property ownership • tax saving

1.1 A BRIEF HISTORY OF EQUITY

1.1.1 The origins of equity

1. Following the Norman Conquest, law was at first administered by the King's Council, the *Curia Regis*.
2. Later, a system of courts was developed with specific jurisdiction.
3. Henry II played major role in developing the legal system and created a professional judiciary, administering courts that dispensed justice on 'circuits' travelling around country, and in a settled bench at Westminster.
4. But common law was formal, slow-moving and highly technical.
5. A variety of significant defects – it was out of need to inject fairness and justice into legal system that equity grew – defects included:
   - the writ system developed so that judges could reach decisions based on established legal reasoning;
   - but became very formalised and maxim 'no remedy without a writ';
   - writ system also depended on 'oral pleading' – which had deficiencies – a mistake in reciting the Latin could lose the action;
   - with growth in number of writs to respond to new 'original' types of action, law became bulky for lawyers who were bound to remember writs for oral pleadings;
   - because of this, Provisions of Oxford 1258 and Statute of Westminster 1285 restricted introduction of new writs – with consequent injustice to potential claimants without a formal claim;
   - use of juries unpredictable as jurors (in trial by presentment, in effect a type of witness) could be bribed or intimidated;
   - common law courts provided only one remedy – damages, or money compensation – often an ineffective

remedy, particularly in the case of interference in a person's property rights;

- common law preoccupied with form – e.g. parol evidence rule.

6. Equity developed to combat deficiencies – initially from disgruntled litigants petitioning the king for fairer answer as 'fountain of all justice'.

7. But extent to which people petitioned him led to delegation of responsibility to the Lord Chancellor – who was a cleric (churchman), and considered to be 'keeper of the king's conscience'.

8. Extent of petitioning led to creation of separate court – Court of Chancery, staffed by clerks of Chancellor – independent court in 1474.

9. Court not bound by writ system – based decisions on fact, not law – and cases heard in English, not Latin.

10. New procedures introduced included:
    - an order for disclosure of documents;
    - a subpoena to compel attendance in court for examination

11. Because Chancery overruled decisions of the common law courts, conflict developed between the two.

12. That decisions were based on discretion was a source of contempt in the common law courts – hence John Sedden's criticism that 'if the measure of equity was the Chancellor's own conscience, one might as well make the standard measure of one foot the Chancellor's foot'.

13. Conflict came to a head in the *Earl of Oxford's case* (1616). Ellesmere incensed Chief Justice Coke of Common Pleas by issuing writs of *habeas corpus*, and the king decided that in conflict, equity would prevail.

14. Eventually, equity became just as formalised as common law and subject to its own technicalities and was heavily criticised in the nineteenth century for excessive delays

15. In the Judicature Acts 1873 and 1875, Court of Chancery became a division of new High Court and equitable

     remedies could be awarded in any court alongside common law remedy of damages.

16. As a result of potential conflict when administering both types of remedies, s25 Judicature Act 1873 provided that in event of a conflict of principles, equitable principle should prevail.

17. So equity defined as 'that body of legal principles built up by the old Court of Chancery, supplemental and superior to the common law'.

18. And equity has been responsible for creating a variety of interests and remedies otherwise unavailable at common law, and is still capable of expanding, e.g. search orders, freezing injunctions.

1.1.2 The equitable maxims

1. The basic character of equity and its key purpose was to introduce fairness and justice into law – on which basis a system of determining the outcome of disputes also evolved, based on reaching a fair solution.

2. These principles guiding judges in a court of equity developed and are known as the maxims of equity – all have to do with fairness.

3. They are guiding principles and so are only followed subject to the discretion of the court – they include:

- **equity acts *in personam*:**
  - an equitable dispute is between the parties;
  - so it will not pass onto a third party.
- **equity looks to the intention not the form:**
  - the classic example is equitable redemption of a mortgage;
  - the purpose of the mortgage is to secure a higher loan than would otherwise be possible;
  - and the mortgagee is protected by being granted beneficial rights in the property by the mortgagor.

- **delay defeats equity:**
  - the equitable equivalent of limitation;
  - if a person seeking an equitable solution to a legal problem fails to bring an action in a reasonable time, he may lose remedy *Allcard v Skinner* (1887); *Leaf v International Galleries* (1950) (both contract law cases)).
- **equity regards that which should be done as being done:**
  - the remedy of specific performance is an obvious example;
  - as is the rule in *Howe v Earl of Dartmouth* (1802) on the duty to act fairly between beneficiaries.
- **equity is equality:**
  - equity tends towards an equal division of property unless the contrary is shown (*Burrough v Philcox* (1840)).
- **he who comes to equity must come with clean hands – and – he who seeks equity must do equity:**
  - both involve the unwillingness of equity to produce a remedy for a party who himself behaves unconscionably;
  - First refers to past conduct - denial of specific performance for trying to take advantage of a mistake in a document of transfer (*Webster v Cecil* (1861));
  - Second demands a basic standard for future conduct – person seeking an injunction to prevent a breach of contract must be prepared to perform his side of the bargain *Chappell v Times Newspapers* (1975)
- **equity will not assist a volunteer:**
  - where there is a covenant to settle property by trust, the trust is only enforceable by those who have provided consideration;
  - however, the rule has some well established exceptions.

- **where equities are equal, the first in time prevails:**
  - whenever trying to assert any equitable right against owner of an existing equitable right.
- **equity will not suffer a wrong to be without a remedy:**
  - includes remedies such as specific performance and injunctions – because damages inadequate;
  - and the trust itself – which allows the beneficial owner to enforce the trust against the legal owner, the trustee.
- **equity will not allow statute to be used as an engine of fraud:**
  - commonly used where to allow a party to rely on a statutory provision is another's detriment, e.g. the requirement of writing in s53 Law of Property Act 1925 (*Bannister v Bannister*);
  - also the basis of the secret trust – trust enforceable despite not conforming to the Wills Act.
- **equity follows the law:**
  - equity acts *in personam* by seeking to prevent injustice, not by replacing or overruling common law;
  - so restrictive covenants enforced to avoid unconscionable behaviour by parties subject to them (and genuine interests of legal owner of land are not interfered with);
  - but positive covenants are not enforced because this would interfere with the common law doctrine of privity (the person trying to enforce the covenant not being a party to it).

1.1.3 Equitable interests (beside the trust)

1. Mortgage
   - equitable redemption of a mortgage allows wider land ownership;

- involves conveyance of equitable interests in property with provision for redemption, i.e. upon repayment of the loan;
- mortgagor can use land purchased as collateral for loan;
- mortgagee holds legal interest in land so loan is protected if mortgagor defaults on loan.

2. Lien:
   - a device of commercial law that again splits proprietary interests;
   - creditor of a debt can legally hold property that is subject to the debt until the debt is paid.

3. Restrictive covenants:
   - a way of retaining proprietary interest over land that has been sold;
   - vendor inserts a covenant with initial purchaser, i.e. preventing use of land for business purposes;
   - all subsequent owners of the land are bound – and all subsequent owners of the vendor's land can enforce the covenant.

4. Easements:
   - a means of securing rights over another person's property;
   - could be, e.g. rights of way – and are enforceable.

1.1.4 Equitable remedies

1. Injunctions:
   - an enforceable order of the court to prevent unjust behaviour, e.g. breach of contract, breach of trust;
   - usually prohibitory rather than mandatory because of the difficulty of overseeing them otherwise;
   - can be final (include all necessary relief), or interim (in advance of trial of the issue).

2. Specific performance:
   - enforceable order of court for contract be carried out, e.g. transfer of land;

- because of difficulty of enforcing, only available where subject of contract is unique, e.g. land; and damages would be inadequate – compare *Ryan v Mutual Tontine (Westminster Chambers) Association* (1893) with *Posner v Scott-Lewis* (1987).

3. Rescission:
   - more of relevance to contracts;
   - where a vitiating factor would make the contract voidable by one party, rescission is a remedy putting the parties back to their pre-contractual position if that is possible to achieve.

4. Rectification:
   - appropriate where a written contract is inaccurate as to the actual terms of the contract;
   - where equitable, court will order a written document to be changed to reflect actual agreement – outcome in *Webster v Cecil* (1861).

5. Account:
   - a trustee must account for all profits made from the position as trustee or for any losses caused to the trust;
   - this is part of the trustee's personal liability.

6. Tracing:
   - tracing is a proprietary remedy;
   - and is a basic means of recovering property belonging to the trust.

1.1.5 The scope for expansion and development

1. Lord Denning in particular thought that there was scope to use equity to continue to add fairness and justice to the law.

2. The 'fair and equitable' cases in implied co-ownership illustrate this, with resulting and constructive trusts used interchangeably.

3. Developments of specific uses for injunctions also show expansion:

- **search orders** – originally Anton Piller orders – originated in *Anton Piller KG v Manufacturing Processes Ltd* (1976) to permit entry to defendant's premises to search for documents that may incriminate the defendant – so subject to strict constraints;
- **freezing injunctions** – originally Mareva injunctions – originated in *Mareva Compania Naviera SA v International Bulk Carriers SA* (1975) as means of preventing defendant from disposing of assets to defeat a judgment – so only awarded subject to strict controls, otherwise may force defendant out of business.

1.2 THE BASIC CHARACTER OF A TRUST

1.2.1 The nature of the trust

1. The trust is an instrument originally devised by equity.
2. It helps to distinguish between legal and beneficial ownership of property and also to protect beneficial interests.
3. Legal title vests in trustees while beneficial entitlement is with beneficiaries (in certain cases, e.g. express co-ownership, these may be the same people).
4. Trustees must carry out requirements of trust according to what is in the trust instrument or according to law.
5. Courts will uphold wishes of settlor/testator and protect legitimate interests of all beneficiaries.
6. Mechanism preserves the justice (equity) of the situation

1.2.2 Definition of a trust

1. A trust is:
   - a legal (equitable) arrangement by which:
     - one person, called settlor/donor (*inter vivos*) or testator (on death);

- transfers title in property (whether realty or personalty);
- to another person(s) called the trustee(s) (the person(s) responsible for administering the trust).
- in doing this the settlor/testator (through the trust instrument), or the courts in certain instances:
  - directs the trustee(s) to hold or use the property;
  - for the benefit of certain persons (donees under an *inter vivos* gift – beneficiaries in inheritance on death);
  - or for the promotion of certain purposes (and with few exceptions these purposes must be charitable).
2. If the trustee(s) undertake(s) to carry out directions of settlor/testator (or of court) then they become subject to a binding legal obligation which equity will enforce.

1.2.3 Classifications of trusts

1. Trusts can be classified in different ways according to context.
2. These include:
   - classification according to **method of creation**:
     - express trusts – created by settlor/testator;
     - implied trusts – created usually by operation of law;
     - statutory trusts – 'trusts of land' under Trusts of Land and Appointment of Trustees Act 1996.
   - classification according to type of beneficiary:
     - private trusts – for individual beneficiaries or classes of beneficiary;
     - public trusts – usually for a purpose, i.e. charities.
   - classification according to the **character of the interest**:
     - fixed trusts – an exact sum identified by the settlor/testator or the residuary estate;
     - discretionary trusts – the interest and the exact distribution of the property is identified by the trustee.

1.2.4 The context in which trusts operate

1. Trusts originated to protect the family interests of absent knights.
2. The simple mechanism of splitting legal and beneficial interests in property has allowed trusts to expand and gain a context in the modern world as a means of responding flexibly to most problems thrown up by property ownership.
3. Different uses of the trust include:
   - pension funds:
     - trust used to protect the fund;
     - and for tax concessions advantage.
   - investment – unit trusts:
     - safer way to invest in shares;
     - because the fund is managed by trustees.
   - security for loans:
     - copying traditional mechanism of mortgage in real property;
     - trusts can be attached to loans generally to protect the loan (*Barclays Bank v Quistclose Investments Ltd* (1968)).
   - voluntary arrangements with creditors:
     - creditors subject to the arrangement can be protected as against other creditors e.g. during liquidation.
   - NHS trusts:
     - users of services are not quite in same position as beneficiaries of a trust;
     - but management and administration of facilities are handled in the same way;
     - created by National Health Service and Community Care Act 1990.
   - trade union funds:
     - s2 trade union and Labour Relations Act 1974;
     - means funds held on trust for benefit of Union (not members).

- co-ownership of land:
  - trust is the accepted method of joint ownership of property;
  - before 1996 as a trust for sale;
  - since the Trusts of Land and Appointment of Trustees Act (TOLATA) 1996 as a trust of land.
- clubs and other unincorporated associations:
  - only incorporation creates a separate legal personality;
  - so if unincorporated, then trust is means of holding property for benefit of members.
- charities:
  - the most common purpose trust;
  - but subject to various requirements.
- non-charitable purpose trusts:
  - can be trusts for monuments or tombs;
  - and specific animals;
  - or the *Re Thompson* exception.
- Protection of minors' interests:
  - Law of Property Act 1925 prevents minors from holding the legal estate of land;
  - originally any gift of land to a minor would create a settlement under Settled Land Act 1925;
  - now it would create a trust of land under TOLATA 1996.
- use of nominees in property transfers:
  - common in larger purchases of shares;
  - used to hide identity of real purchaser.
- protective trusts:
  - devised to allow a financially inept beneficiary to have some control over the property;
  - while trustees will ensure that the trust fund does not suffer.
- secret trusts:
  - can be fully secret or half secret;
  - but in either case trust hides identity of the beneficiary.

- preserving wealth:
  - trusts can be used to keep intact a body of wealth that otherwise may be dissipated.
- disputes over property ownership:
  - courts may intervene using implied trusts;
  - to distribute ownership fairly.
- tax saving:
  - placing property in trust is a common tax saving device;
  - example is avoiding inheritance tax.

CHAPTER 2

THE CREATION OF EXPRESS PRIVATE TRUSTS

Capacity:
- Children – settlements are voidable – cannot hold land other than behind a trust
- Mentally incapacitated – protected by Court of Protection under s95 Mental Health Act 1983 – and can create trusts (*Re Bearley*)

Trusts of land:
- Testamentary requirements of Wills Act
- Words used must be capable of forming trust
- s53 LPA 1925 requires proof in writing
- s2 Law of Property (Miscellaneous Provisions) Act 1989 requires actual written document incorporating all of terms (*Firstpast Homes v Johnson*)

CREATION OF EXPRESS PRIVATE TRUSTS

Disposition of existing equitable interests:
- by s53 (l)(c) must be in writing or disposition void
- problem is what amounts to a disposition – most likely given natural meaning (*Grey v IRC*)
- some actions do not count as dispositions, e.g. disclaimer of a beneficial interest (*Re Paradise Motor Co*)
- where sole owner disposes of legal and equitable title together no written disposition needed (*Vandervell v IRC*)
- position of specifically performable contracts is more problematic (*Oughtread v IRC*)

The three certainties:
Trust must be expressed in such a way that the testator's instructions can be carried out.
Certainty of intention:
- words should express an imperative obligation (*Wright v Atkyns*)
- so if words demonstrate a different obligation no trust is created (*Jones v Lock*)
- precatory words, e.g. 'hope', 'desire' may be too uncertain for trust to succeed (*Re Adams and the Kensington Vestry*) – but see *Comisky v Bowring-Hanbury*

Certainty of subject matter:
- gift must be precisely identified – so 'remaining part of what is left' would fail (*Sprange v Barnard*)
- position on shares is different (*Re London Wine Co (Shippers)*)
- court may use objective standard in deciding what comes within gift (*Re Golay's*)

Certainty of objects:
- the beneficiaries should be clearly identified – or if part of a class 'list principle' applies (*Re Endacott*)
- trustees may use 'Benjamin orders' for protection when distributing funds
- in discretionary trusts 'any given postulant' test is used – based on conceptual and evidential certainty (*McPhail v Doulton*);
- unless class is too large then uses 'administrative workability' test (*R v District Auditor ex parte West Yorkshire County Council*).

2.1 CAPACITY AND THE CREATION OF TRUSTS

1. Capacity to create a trust usually goes hand in hand with the ability to hold or dispose of legal or equitable interests.
2. So two specific instances of parties lacking capacity to create a trust:
   - children – minors under age 18:
     - any settlement is voidable;
     - children cannot hold a legal estate in land – so any land comes to a child behind a trust.
   - mentally incapacitated:
     - ability to create a trust is limited by the size of the gift and relationship with assets owned (*Re Beaney* (1978));
     - Court of Protection can produce settlement for a mentally incapacitated person by virtue of s95 Mental Health Act 1983 – guiding principle being what would the person him/herself do if not incapacitated (*Re T.B.* (1967)).

2.2 FORMALITIES – GENERAL

1. To create a lifetime gift of land – must conform to s53 Law of Property Act 1925 and the 'three certainties'.
2. S53 requires written evidence for land – no requirement for personalty.
3. If gift is testamentary, additional requirements in Wills Act 1837, as amended, must be followed – written form, signing, witnessing etc.
4. Words used must also always be capable of creating a trust.
5. All the above applies to express trusts but not resulting or constructive.

2.3 TRUSTS OF LAND

1. Land inevitably requires special formalities – as it does in law of real property.

2. In the case of trusts of land, two specific provisions are significant:
   - by s53(1)(b) LPA 1925 'A declaration of trust respecting any land or any interest therein must be manifested and proved by some writing signed by the person who is able to declare such a trust or by his will';
   - by s2 Law of Property (Miscellaneous Provisions) Act 1989 contracts for disposition of land 'can only be made in writing and only by incorporating all of the terms which the parties have expressly agreed in one document' – so dispositions of land, including trust, are void if not written (*Firstpost Homes v Johnson* (1995)).

2.4 DISPOSITIONS OF EXISTING EQUITABLE INTERESTS

1. By s53(1)(c) LPA 1925 'A disposition of an equitable interest or trust subsisting at the time of the disposition must be in writing signed by the person disposing of the same or by his agent thereto lawfully authorised in writing or by will.'

2. So failure to comply means disposition is void.

3. Key question is what amounts to a 'disposition'.

4. Most cases on meaning of disposition involve tax avoidance schemes – so not surprising that courts take a tough line.

5. Case law suggests that the word 'disposition' is to be given its natural meaning (*Grey v IRC* (1957)) – so oral instructions will count as a failed disposition for lack of written form.

6. However, where a sole owner disposes of both legal and equitable title simultaneously there may be no need for a written disposition of the equitable interest as long as the

formalities for the legal estate are complied with (*Vandervell v IRC* (1967)).

7. An assignment of an equitable interest is straightforwardly a disposition and will be void unless in writing

8. However, certain actions appear not to be dispositions e.g.:
   - a disclaimer of a beneficial interest (*Re Paradise Motor Co* (1968));
   - nominations under a staff pension scheme (*Re Danish Bacon Co Staff Pension Fund Trusts* (1971));
   - a declaration by a beneficiary that he holds his beneficial interest for someone else.

9. The much more difficult question concerns the position of specifically enforceable contracts for sale – here the main emphasis may be on preventing tax avoidance rather than following technicalities absolutely (*Oughtred v IRC* (1960)).

2.5 FORMALITY AND FRAUD

1. One further key issue is whether or not a trust can be set aside to avoid sanctioning fraud.

2. Two equitable maxims may apply:
   - equity looks to the intention and not the form;
   - equity will not allow statute to be used as a cloak of fraud.

3. It has been held possible to set aside operation of s53(1)(b) in order to avoid obvious fraud (*Rochefoucauld v Boustead* (1897)).

4. A further example of equity acting to prevent a fraud is the secret trust.

2.6 THE THREE CERTAINTIES

2.6.1 Introduction

1. For a trust to be formed, settlor must make intentions absolutely clear.

2. So the trust must be sufficiently clear for trustee to carry out all instructions and for court to be able to enforce it against trustee.

3. So, besides statutory formalities, creation of an express private trust depends on the presence of the 'three certainties':
   - certainty of intention – the words creating a binding obligation;
   - certainty of subject matter – the property subject to the trust;
   - certainty of objects – the beneficiaries.

4. But certainty has entirely different meaning in relation to purpose trusts.

5. In all cases there is interrelationship between the three and certainty is a question of construction for the courts.

2.6.2 Certainty of intention

1. The most significant point is that the 'words must be imperative' Lord Eldon in (*Wright v Atkyns* (1823)).

2. The words must make clear that trustee is under a binding obligation.

3. The best words are clearly 'to hold upon trust for' – but the word 'trust' is not vital – Megarry J in *Re Kayford* (1975).

4. Only sufficient intention to create a trust must be shown (*Paul v Constance* (1977)).

5. If the words demonstrate a different intention then there is no trust created (*Jones v Lock* (1865)).

6. A further difficulty concerns use of 'precatory' words, e.g. 'hope', 'desire'.

7. Traditionally, it was accepted that these could still create a trust – but a turning point came in *Lambe v Eames* (1871).

8. And they are generally now taken to be too uncertain to create a trust (*Re Adams and the Kensington Vestry* (1884)).

9. But context is all important and it is still possible to construe a trust from precatory words if sufficient intention can be found (*Comiskey v Bowring-Hanbury* (1905)).

10. Specific words accepted in the past as creating or not creating a trust can act as precedents (*Re Steele's Will Trusts* (1948)).

11. But courts only accept trust intended to be acted upon – and reject a sham covering an ulterior purpose (*Midland Bank plc v Wyatt* (1995)).

2.6.3 Certainty of subject matter

1. Almost anything can form the subject matter of a trust – but the property settled must be identified precisely.

2. So many examples of choice of words that failed to create a trust:
   - 'the bulk of my estate' (*Palmer v Simmonds* (1854));
   - 'such parts of my estate as she shall not have sold' (*Re Jones* (1898));
   - 'the remaining part of what is left' (*Sprange v Barnard* (1789)).

3. In the case of chattels if the specific property is not identified then, as is the case with commercial law where property will not pass, neither will a trust be created (*Re Goldcorp Exchange Ltd* (1994)).

4. Although quite different problems are created where the property is shares (*Hunter v Moss* (1994)).

5. So the position is different (*Re London Wine Co (Shippers)* (1986)).

6. Absence of certainty of subject matter can have two possible results:
   - the gift goes absolutely to the first donee;
   - the gift fails and falls on resulting trust back to the settlor's estate (*Sprange v Barnard* (1789)).

7. One further problem, besides identifying what property comes within the trust, is how it is distributed between

beneficiaries – in which the court might use an objective standard (*Re Golay's Will Trusts* (1965)).
8. But if division of property left to discretion of specific individual who can no longer exercise discretion then gift fails (*Boyce v Boyce* (1849)).

2.6.4 Certainty of objects

1. In fixed trusts (i.e. where obligation is to named beneficiaries or to all members of a named class), trustees must know the precise identities of the objects – known as the 'list principle' (*Re Endacott* (1959)).
2. The general rule is that the description of the beneficiaries should be neither conceptually nor evidentially uncertain – otherwise gift will fail.
3. To avoid unfairness when the class is certain but individual members cannot be found the courts have developed the 'Benjamin order' from *Re Benjamin* (1902) – this authorises distribution to known beneficiaries and missing beneficiaries then claim against existing beneficiaries rather than against the trustees.
4. The rule on certainty of objects should be no wider than necessary to allow the trustees to undertake their duties properly.
5. Traditionally, with discretionary trusts, same rule applied – beneficiaries must all be identifiable (*IRC v Broadway Cottage Trust* (1955)).
6. In *McPhail v Doulton* (1971) the position was examined in detail since with the size of the apparent class of beneficiaries equal distribution would have been completely impracticable:
   • the court adopted the 'any given postulant test' derived from rules on powers in *Re Gulbenkian* (1968): 'power is valid if it can be said with certainty whether any given individual is or is not a member of the class and does not fail simply because it is impossible to ascertain every member of the class';

- in analysing test CA (in *Re Baden's Deed Trusts (No 2)*
  (1972)) distinguished between conceptual and
  evidential certainty:
    - 'conceptual' means precise definition of class settlor
      wishes to benefit – without which gift fails;
    - 'evidential' means extent to which evidentially a
      person can be included in the class – complete
      certainty virtually impossible;
- court accepted that some people would definitely come
  within class and some would definitely fall outside it –
  in the case of others they would fall outside class unless
  they could prove they were within it;
- it is of course possible for a class to be so wide that it
  could not be upheld even though both conceptual and
  evidential certainty tests from *McPhail v Doulton*
  possible – then court suggested a further test of
  'administrative workability – since applied in *R v
  District Auditor ex parte West Yorkshire County Council*
  (1998).

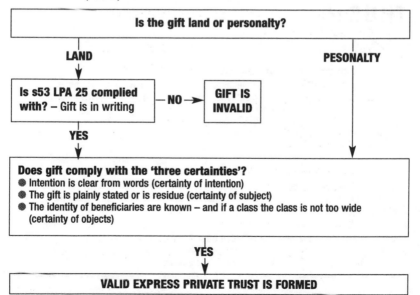

Diagram illustrating the major requirements for valid formation of express private trusts

CHAPTER 3

PURPOSE TRUSTS

Objections to purpose trusts:
- Lack of certainty (*Morice v Bishop of Durham*).
- Lack of ascertainable beneficiaries – so needs residuary beneficiary.
- Offends perpetuity – so only valid if expressed to fall inside period.
- Policy reasons, e.g. should not involve capricious expenditure (*McCaig's Trustees*).

Accepted non-charitable purpose trusts:
Upkeep of tombs and monuments:
- E.g. for a family enclosure (*Pirbright v Salway*).
- If involves moderate expenditure (*McCaig*); certain (*Re Endacott*); and satisfies perpetuity rule (*Re Hooper*).
Maintenance of specific animals:
- Will fail test for charitable purpose (*Pettingall v Pettingall*).
- Valid if perpetuity rule met (*Re Dean*).
Saying of masses:
- Private masses fail charity tests.
- But upheld here (*Bourne v Keane*).
Re Thompson (foxhunting):
- Major anomaly – unlikely to be followed.

PURPOSE TRUSTS

The rules on unincorporated associations:
- Two or more people joined for 'common purposes ... each having mutual duties ... in an organisation [with] rules which identify ... control of it...funds ... (*Conservative and Unionist Central Office v Burrell*).
- Question of what happens to gifts to such associations decided in *Neville Estates v Madden* – gift is to existing members ... subject to their respective contractual rights and liabilities towards one another.
- But gift fails if rules offend perpetuity period or rules prevent members from ending association and dividing fund *Re Lipinski's Will Trusts*.
- So each member has contractual obligations to prevent misapplication of gift – and committee members are also bound by rules which may be enforced against them.
- Alternative is that gift is purely for members but difficulty is that members must be ascertainable *Re Denly's Trust Deed*.
- Distribution originally based on resulting trust *Re Printers' and Transferrers' Amalgamated Trades Protection Society* but now on contract basis above *Re The Sick and Funeral Society of St John's Sunday School Golcan*.

3.1 NON-CHARITABLE PURPOSE TRUSTS

3.1.1 General

1. A private trust is a trust in favour of ascertainable beneficiaries.
2. A charitable trust, on the other hand, is a trust for purposes which according to established tests is accepted as charitable and thus exempt from certain requirements of express private trusts.
3. Non-charitable purpose trusts fall outside of either category above.
4. They do not get the benefits accorded to charitable trusts – but in certain cases may be upheld as valid.
5. One logic of accepting such categories of trusts is that, while they are expressed as being for purposes, they can still possibly be construed as being for the benefit of individuals affected by the purpose (*Re Denly's Trust Deed* (1969)).
6. But, the same logic cannot be applied where the class of beneficiaries is too wide and therefore makes the trust 'administratively unworkable' (*R v District Auditor ex parte West Yorkshire Metropolitan County Council* (1986)).

3.1.2 The objections to having purpose trusts

1. Traditionally there was no absolute prohibition on the creation of non-charitable purposes – but a rule was developed in *Re Endacott* (1960).
2. Traditionally such trusts failed because of defects in their creation, eg:
   - lack of certainty;
   - lack of an ascertainable beneficiary;
   - offending the perpetuity period;
   - excess delegation of testamentary powers.

3. Certainty:
   * all trusts need certainty – and a non-charitable purpose trust is no exception;
   * so the purpose must be 'stated in phrases which embody definite concepts and the means by which the trustees are to try to attain them must also be prescribed with a sufficient degree of certainty' (Roxburgh J in *Re Astor* (1952));
   * the trust is only valid if expressed with sufficient certainty for court to control performance (*Morice v Bishop of Durham* (1804)).

4. Ascertainable beneficiaries:
   * many purpose trusts may indirectly benefit individuals – but unless these rank as ascertainable beneficiaries then the trust fails – as Grant MR identifies in *Morice*;
   * it follows that there can be no obligation on the trustees without a corresponding right enjoyed by an identifiable beneficiary;
   * in the case of private trusts these are named beneficiaries – and in charitable trusts the Attorney-General.

5. The perpetuity rule:
   * the rule has two aspects: (i) no gift should fall outside the perpetuity period; (ii) no gift should last for longer than the perpetuity period;
   * the point of the rule at common law was originally to avoid tying up land for excessive periods and the uncertainty such gifts could create;
   * the original perpetuity period at common law was – the life in being plus 21 years (the life in being was some person alive at the time of the gift – and the gift would fail if it could vest outside of the 21-year period, e.g. 'To the first child of A to reach the age of 25');
   * so non-charitable purpose trusts failed if could fall outside period;
   * common law rule is modified by Perpetuities and Accumulations Act 1964 – this Act allows the settlor to

specify a period of no more than 80 years, and introduces the principle of 'wait and see' (i.e. wait to see if gift vests outside of period before invalidating it).

6. Policy:
   - the courts may invalidate a gift which they feel is capricious or an inappropriate way of spending the money (*M'Caig's Trustees v The Kirk Session of the United Free Church of Lismore* (1915));
   - delegation of testamentary power has also been challenged in (*Leahy v A-G for New South Wales* but accepted in *Re Beatty's Will Trusts* (1990)).

3.1.3 Exceptions to the rule against non-charitable purpose trusts

1. Despite valid objections to purpose trusts some exceptions exist.
2. They are generally referred to as 'trusts of imperfect obligation' – are anomalous, and fall into a limited range of specific exceptions.
3. Trusts for tombs and monuments:
   - it is valid to provide a gift for creation and upkeep of a family enclosure (*Pirbright v Salway* (1896));
   - a gift may also succeed in respect of monuments to persons other than the testator (*Mussett v Bingle* (1876));
   - but the courts will only usually accept the use of quite moderate sums of money for such gifts (*M'Caig*);
   - as usual, a gift fails for any lack of certainty (*Re Endacott* (1960));
   - and in any case a gift is only valid if falling inside the perpetuity period (*Re Hooper* (1932)).
4. Trusts for the maintenance of specific animals:
   - a trust for animals generally can succeed as charitable if certain conditions are met;

- a trust for an individual animal must necessarily fail as a charitable gift – but might still be upheld as a non-charitable purpose trust (*Pettingall v Pettingall* (1842));
- but not if such a gift offends perpetuity (*Re Dean* (1889));
- the perpetuity period must refer to human lives (*Re Kelly* (1932)).

5. Trusts for the saying of masses:
   - a mass said in public place will generally be upheld as charitable (*Re Hetherington* (1989));
   - but a gift for purely private religious ceremonies cannot be classed as charitable (*Re Le Cren Clarke* (1996));
   - but this does not always matter since trusts for the saying of purely private masses have been upheld as valid purpose trusts (*Bourne v Keane* (1919)).

6. The *Re Thompson* exception (a trust for foxhunting):
   - a strange gift upheld as valid because of a residuary beneficiary;
   - it was also upheld because the purpose was certain;
   - but it ranks as a major anomaly – and unlikely to be followed.

3.1.4 The modern position

1. In *Re Astor's Settlement Trusts* (1952) it was suggested that all the exceptions are merely 'concessions to human weakness or sentiment'.
2. In *Re Endacott* (1960) it was also noted that they are 'troublesome, anomalous and aberrant'.
3. It is thus unlikely that they will be extended in any way.
4. However, the development of the discretionary trust in *McPhail v Doulton* (1971) has been said to have 'broken the stranglehold imposed on the development of trusts'.

3.2 THE RULES ON UNINCORPORATED ASSOCIATIONS

3.2.1 The nature of unincorporated associations

1. An unincorporated association is a joining together of two or more people for 'common purposes by mutual undertakings, each having mutual duties and obligations in an organisation which has rules which identify in whom control of it and its funds rests and on what terms and which may be joined or left at will' (*Conservative and Unionist Central Office v Burrell* (1982)).

2. Such associations lack the formal creation of incorporation so have no separate legal personality so cannot hold property in their own right or be the subject of rights and obligations in their own names.

3. The common classes of such groups include – sports and social clubs, cultural groups, and certain charitable bodies.

4. Such groups can still be the beneficiaries of gifts and also are required to handle funds – so a number of significant problems arise:
   * what happens to gifts made to these associations?
   * how do these associations hold funds or property?
   * what happens to funds on dissolution of the association?

3.2.2 Gifts made to unincorporated associations

1. If an association is charitable and a gift is for the association's purposes then it is taken as *prima facie* for charitable purposes – the usual rules on certainty do not apply and even when the association ceases to exist the gift can be saved by the *cy-près* doctrine.

2. If the association is not charitable then the gift is void as a purpose trust unless falling under the very limited exceptions.

3. If a gift cannot take effect as a gift on trust for the purposes of the association then the question arises how such gifts can take effect and whether or not they can take effect as gifts to the members.

4. Originally it was thought that there was no need to identify who would be the beneficiaries – as long as persons holding the gift as trustees had the power to spend any money (*Re Drummond* (1914)).

5. The different possible outcomes were considered in *Neville Estates v Madden* (1961) where Cross J identified three possible categories:
   - 'a gift to the members ... at the relevant date ... so that any ... can sever his share and claim it' (a gift to present members);
   - 'a gift to the existing members ... subject to their respective contractual rights and liabilities towards one another' (a gift to members subject to the constitutional rules of the association as to members' rights and liabilities);
   - 'a gift ... at the disposal of the members for the time being ... held in trust' (a gift on trust for members)

6. Where the trust instrument only states that the gift is to the association then *prima facie* it may be construed as a gift for the members (*Leahy v A-G for New South Wales* (1959)).

7. It is easier to see the first of Cross J's three categories as acceptable if the gift identifies clearly a limited class of persons who may benefit from it (*Re Denly's Trust Deed* (1969)).

8. The third of Cross J's three categories throws up a number of other points of note:
   - that the trust mechanism is inappropriate if it is clear that the members are not intended to benefit from the gift;
   - that the gift, unless charitable, will fail unless limited by the perpetuity period;

- also that gift cannot be to members if rules of association actually prescribe against that eventuality (*Re Grant's Will Trusts* (1980)).

9. The most plausible of the three alternatives is the second, that gift takes effect as a gift to the members of the association subject to their contractual rights and liabilities to one another – and it is this solution that causes the least problems (*Re Recher's Will Trusts* (1971)).

10. On this basis, question as to whether or not the gift is subject to any restrictions on its use depends on intentions of association as to the relationship of its members rather than on explicit intention of settlor. The gift will fail if rules of association offend perpetuity period or if members are prevented by rules from ending association and dividing the funds amongst themselves (*Re Lipinski's Will Trusts* (1976)).

3.2.3 Funds held by unincorporated associations

1. The problems are exactly the same as those identified above.

2. Again, the 'contractual solution' is the best.

3. Each member, therefore, has contractual obligations to prevent the misapplication of the gift – and committee members are also bound by the rules of the association which may be enforced against them.

4. The alternative based on trust poses the obvious problem that a trust cannot generally be held for purposes unless charitable.

5. The alternative that the gift is purely for the members again has the difficulty that the members must be ascertainable, as in *Re Denly's*.

6. Other problems, of course, still exist – e.g. if the gift is one of land rather than chattels.

3.2.4 Distribution of the fund

1. A final problem is what happens to the fund if the association is wound up.
2. Many of the used solutions appear at odds with the reasoning above.
3. The general rule traditionally was that funds were held on resulting trust for members according to their contribution (*Re Printers' and Transferrers' Amalgamated Trades Protection Society* (1899)).
4. More modern approach is to follow contract argument – the logic of using resulting trusts is at odds with argument that gift is outright gift to members subject to the rules of the association (*Re The Sick and Funeral Society of St John's Sunday School Golcan* (1972)).

CHAPTER 4
CONSTITUTION OF TRUSTS

Formalities
- Trust complete if settlor is also trustee – but if other trustees then incomplete till property passed to them.
- Transfer and formalities must be by prescribed method.
- Chattels = delivery (*Thomas v Times Books*).
- Cheques = endorsement (*Jones v Lock*).
- Land by conveyance.
- Copyright = written transfer.
- Shares = share transfer form and registration (*Milroy v Loro* – but see also *Re Rose*).

Declaration of self as trustee:
- Must be evidence of intention to create trust.
- For land would need written evidence.
- Otherwise no particular words needed (*Jones v Lock*).
- May show intention to hold for benefit of third party (*Paul v Constance*).

CONSTITUTION OF TRUSTS

Enforcement of trusts:
- Gratutious statement of intention not binding.
- If more formal – then depends on whether volunteer or non-volunteer.
- Equity will not assist a volunteer, i.e. one not giving valuable consideration.
- Includes person covered by marriage settlement (*Pullan v Koe*).
- If beneficiary is party to covenant in a deed then common law action for damages possible (*Cannon v Hartley*).
- Or Contracts (Rights of Third Parties) Act 1999 possible.
- Generally felt that trustees cannot enforce covenant on behalf of volunteers (*Re Kay's Settlement*).
- If trustees seeks damages instead of specific performance then may succeed (*Re Cavendish-Browne*).
- And also argued that promise may create trust (*Fletcher v Fletcher*).

Exceptions to the rule that equity will not assist a volunteer:
The rule in *Strong v Bird*:
- Incomplete gift made during settlor's lifetime and donee made executor then gift complete – beneficiaries have no claim.

Donatio mortis causa (deathbed gift):
- Must be made in contemplation of death (*Wilkes v Allington*); and
- Subject matter passed to donee (*Sen v Hedley*); and
- Gift made in circumstances that show it will revert to donor if he recovers.

Proprietary estoppel:
- A person led to act in reliance on promise made by other person – then person making promise cannot go back on it.
- So sometimes creates a proprietary interest in favour of a volunteer (*Crabb v Arun UDC*).

4.1 GENERAL

1. If the settlor creates a trust by declaring himself as trustee then:
   - trust is complete and beneficiaries may acquire rights in property;
   - providing both formalities and certainty is satisfied;
   - because property will already be vested in the trustees.
2. But if settlor intends to create trust by transferring property to other trustees then:
   - the trust is incomplete until he does so;
   - and the trust is unenforceable by beneficiaries until he does so.

4.2 FORMALITIES

1. Turner LJ in *Milroy v Lord* (1862): 'to render a voluntary settlement effectual the settlor must have done everything which, according to the nature of the property comprised in the settlement, was necessary in order to transfer the property and render the settlement binding'.
2. Formalities and transfer must be according to prescribed method.
3. With chattels delivery is sufficient (*Thomas v Times Books* (1966)).
4. With cheques, endorsement is needed (*Jones v Lock* (1865)).
5. Deed of gift is the surest way.
6. Land needs conveyance in form of a deed (LPA 1925 and LP(MP)A 1989).
7. Copyright needs transfer in writing.
8. Shares need completion of share transfer forms and registration (*Milroy v Lord* (1862)) – though a contradictory position was taken in *Re Rose* (1952) – followed in trust context in *Hunter v Moss* (1999).

4.3 DECLARATION OF SELF AS TRUSTEE

1. While settlor must transfer property to trustees by appropriate method – there must also be evident an intention to create a trust.
2. This need only be a clear intention (but for land would require writing).
3. Specific words declaring the trust are unnecessary if intention that one party holds as trustee for another's benefit is shown (*Jones v Lock*).
4. In contrast to above is situation where owner has not transferred property to third party but has shown that he intends to hold for benefit of the third party (*Paul v Constance* (1977)).

4.4 ENFORCEMENT OF TRUSTS – VOLUNTEERS AND NON-VOLUNTEERS

1. If a settlor merely makes a gratuitous oral statement of intention to create a trust then this is not binding.
2. If, however, settlor's intention is demonstrated by more formal means, e.g. written covenant to transfer property then enforceability may depend on whether intended beneficiary is volunteer or non-volunteer.
3. Equity will generally not assist a volunteer.
4. A volunteer in this context is one not providing valuable consideration.
5. But in equity this can include a person covered by a marriage settlement (*Pullan v Koe* (1913)).
6. A marriage settlement includes spouses, children (who are said to be coated with consideration) and sometimes also e.g. step children – if there is a sufficiently close relationship – but it will not cover next of kin generally (*Re Plumptree's Marriage Settlement* (1910)).

7. Since enforcement depends on specific performance of the covenant – then the property must also be of a type to which specific performance can apply (*Pullan v Koe*).

8. But if one of intended beneficiaries is a party to covenant in a deed – then whether that person is a volunteer or not, common law may provide an action for damages for breach of covenant even though specific performance is unavailable (*Cannon v Hartley* (1949)).

9. Now Contracts (Rights of Third Parties) Act 1999 available sometimes.

10. But for enforcement of covenants made before Act another issue is whether trustees can enforce covenant on behalf of volunteers – courts have been unwilling to accept this possibility (*Re Pryce* (1917)).

11. But have suggested that trustees cannot pursue such a course of action (*Re Kay's Settlement* (1939)).

12. And trustees 'could not and should not seek to enforce covenants on behalf of volunteers' (*Re Cooke's Settlement Trusts* (1964)).

13. But if a trustee seeks damages instead of enforcement then they may succeed (*Re Cavendish-Browne's Settlement Trusts* (1916)).

14. A final way of trustee assisting volunteer in unique circumstances is to argue that, once a promise has been made to settle property that this itself is subject of an enforceable trust (*Fletcher v Fletcher* (1844)).

4.5 EXCEPTIONS TO THE RULE THAT EQUITY WILL NOT ASSIST A VOLUNTEER

1. The rule in *Strong v Bird* (1874):
   - if incomplete gift made during donor's lifetime and donee then made executor to donor's will gift is completed and beneficiaries have no claim on property;

- But vagueness of intention defeats the rule *Re Gonin (1979)*

2. *Donatio mortis causa* (gift made in contemplation of death):
   - In *Cain v Moon* (1896) Lord Russell CJ set basic requirements:
     (i) the gift must have been made in contemplation of death (*Wilkes v Allington* (1931));
     (ii) subject matter must have been passed to donee e.g. freehold land (*Sen v Headley* (1991)); chattels – delivery (*Woodward v Woodward* (1992)); choses in action – necessary documents (*Birch v Treasury Solicitor* (1951));
     (iii) the gift must be made in such circumstances that show that the property will revert to the donor should he recover.

3. Proprietary estoppel
   - if one person has been led to act on statement of another, he may in some circumstances prevent other from going back on promise;
   - but sometimes doctrine has effect of creating a proprietary interest in favour of a volunteer – see *Dillwynn v Llewellyn* (1862) and *Crabb v Arun UDC* (1976).

CHAPTER 5

SECRET TRUSTS

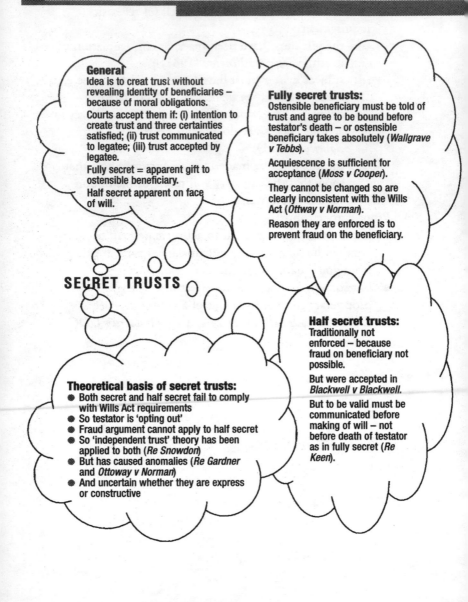

General
Idea is to creat trust without revealing identity of beneficiaries – because of moral obligations.

Courts accept them if: (i) intention to create trust and three certainties satisfied; (ii) trust communicated to legatee; (iii) trust accepted by legatee.

Fully secret = apparent gift to ostensible beneficiary.

Half secret apparent on face of will.

Fully secret trusts:
Ostensible beneficiary must be told of trust and agree to be bound before testator's death – or ostensible beneficiary takes absolutely (*Wallgrave v Tebbs*).

Acquiescence is sufficient for acceptance (*Moss v Cooper*).

They cannot be changed so are clearly inconsistent with the Wills Act (*Ottway v Norman*).

Reason they are enforced is to prevent fraud on the beneficiary.

SECRET TRUSTS

Half secret trusts:
Traditionally not enforced – because fraud on beneficiary not possible.

But were accepted in *Blackwell v Blackwell*.

But to be valid must be communicated before making of will – not before death of testator as in fully secret (*Re Keen*).

Theoretical basis of secret trusts:
- Both secret and half secret fail to comply with Wills Act requirements
- So testator is 'opting out'
- Fraud argument cannot apply to half secret
- So 'independent trust' theory has been applied to both (*Re Snowdon*)
- But has caused anomalies (*Re Gardner* and *Ottoway v Norman*)
- And uncertain whether they are express or constructive

5.1 THE BACKGROUND TO SECRET TRUSTS

1. A will is a public document – so can be read by anyone.
2. This can cause problems for testators who wish to keep the identity of certain beneficiaries secret, e.g. because of moral obligations to them.
3. One traditional answer was to make an absolute gift to an 'ostensible beneficiary' who was instructed as to the real purpose of the gift (the fully secret trust) – and equity would prevent the ostensible beneficiary's unjust enrichment and enforce the trust.
4. A further way is to identify that person as a trustee in the will but still not reveal the identity of the secret beneficiary, i.e. 'to X for purposes which I have made known to him' (the half secret trust) – the gift being immediately enforceable as there is no question of the trustee taking it.
5. Secret trusts are potentially problematic because their exact nature is unclear and because they do not meet the requirements of certain formalities – s9 Will Act 1837.
6. But courts do still approve of secret trusts if there is '(i) an intention by the testator to create a trust, satisfying the traditional requirements of the three certainties; (ii) communication of the trust to the legatees; (iii) acceptance of the trust by the legatees … which … can take the form of silent acquiescence …' (Nourse LJ in *Margulies v Margulies* (2000)).

5.2 THE RULES GOVERNING FULLY SECRET TRUSTS

1. The ostensible beneficiary must be informed of the trust and agree to be bound by it before the testator's death – so the trust must be communicated or the ostensible beneficiary will take absolutely (*Wallgrave v Tebbs* (1855)).

2. The ostensible beneficiary must be told of the terms of the trust as well as of the existence of the trust (*Re Boyes* (1884)).

3. The trust can be communicated orally or in writing, and could be in sealed instructions to be opened after death (*Re Keen* (1937)).

4. Acceptance of the trust does not have to be formal – silence or acquiescence is sufficient (*Moss v Cooper* (1861)).

5. The ostensible beneficiary must be informed of changes or additions to the trust or (s)he will take them absolutely (*Re Colin Cooper* (1939)).

6. It has also proved possible for a testator to use a secret trust to create an obligation on the ostensible beneficiary to make provision on his/her death for the secret beneficiary (*Re Gardner (No 1)* (1920)).

7. Creating clear inconsistencies with normal rules on wills, i.e. a secret trust cannot be altered where a will can (*Ottaway v Norman* (1972)).

8. The original justification for secret trusts was preventing any fraud by the ostensible beneficiary – in which case the standard of proof should be high as for fraud (*Ottaway v Norman*) – but Megarry V-C has suggested that either oral or written proof is sufficient and that the standard of proof is only the normal civil measure (*Re Snowden* (1979)).

5.3 THE RULES GOVERNING HALF SECRET TRUSTS

1. Courts traditionally had greater difficulty in accepting half secret trusts.

2. The rationale for fully secret trusts – prevention of fraud by the ostensible beneficiary – clearly cannot apply since a trust is created on the face of the will and there would never be any question of the trustee taking the property absolutely.

3. Traditionally, then, it was argued that there was no reason not to demand compliance with the requirements of the Wills Act 1837 – so half secret trusts were commonly not enforced and returned instead on resulting trust to the testators' estate.

4. But half secret trusts were eventually accepted as valid in *Blackwell v Blackwell* (1929) where Lord Sumner stated that 'it is communication of the purpose to the legatee coupled with acquiescence or promise on his part that removes the matter from the provisions of the Wills Act and brings it within the law of trusts'.

5. However, as Lord Sumner also identified *obiter*: '... a testator cannot reserve to himself a power to make future unwitnessed dispositions by merely naming a trust and leaving the purposes of the trust to be supplied afterwards'.

6. So there is clear inconsistency in the relative positions on communication in fully secret trusts and half secret trusts – the former communication need only be before the testator's death – but with the latter it must be at or before the making of the will (*Re Keen* (1937)).

5.4 THE THEORETICAL BASIS OF SECRET TRUSTS

1. While there are good reasons why testators use secret trusts and why courts will enforce them – they are still problematic.

2. Both fully secret and half secret trusts fail to comply with necessary formalities in the Wills Act.

3. The traditional justification for allowing secret trusts to disregard statutory requirements is the equitable maxim – equity will not allow statute to be used as an engine of fraud.

4. This fraud theory obviously applies in the case of fully secret trusts but cannot apply to half secret trusts where a

trust is apparent on the face of the will and there is no possibility of the trustee keeping the property.

5. Also the view of Lord Sumner in *Blackwell v Blackwell* that secret trusts are based on 'intention, communication, and acquiescence' is insufficient justification on its own because this has the effect of allowing a testator to 'contract out' of the provisions of the Wills Act – to choose to avoid statutory provision.

6. The more modern view is that both fully secret and half secret trusts operate outside of the will so have no need to comply with the provisions of the Wills Act – as Megarry V-C points out in *Re Snowden*: 'The whole basis of secret trusts ... is that they operate outside of the will, changing nothing that is written in it, and allowing it to operate according to its tenor, but then fastening a trust onto the property in the hands of the recipient'.

7. So a major justification for the 'independent trust theory' is still based on the personal obligation accepted by the ostensible beneficiary (*Re Young* (1951)).

8. But the principle has led to some dramatic and controversial results (*Re Gardner* (1923)).

9. One final point is whether the secret trust operates as a constructive trust or as an express trust:
   - in the case of half secret trusts, they can only ever be express as the trust is apparent on the face of the will;
   - in the case of fully secret trusts, either could apply;
   - if they are a means of avoiding formal requirements of the Wills Act to prevent fraud by the ostensible beneficiary, then they would operate as constructive trusts;
   - if they operate independently of the will, then they must be regarded as express trusts;
   - the significance is in whether or not s53(1)(b) must be complied with in the case of a trust of land – it need not be in a constructive trust – but in *Ottaway v Norman* an oral fully secret trust of land was upheld without the issue being discussed.

Fully secret trusts	Half secret trusts
Are created to benefit a 'secret' beneficiary.	Are created to benefit a 'secret' beneficiary.
Are not apparent on the face of the will.	Are apparent on the face of the will.
Do not fulfil certain requirements of the Wills Act.	Do not fulfil certain requirements of the Wills Act.
Secret trustee (ostensible beneficiary) must be informed before testator's death of existence and terms of trust – and must accept.	Secret trustee is identified on face of will – and must be informed before will is made – and accept or acquiesce.
If trust fails then ostensible beneficiary takes gift absolutely.	If trust fails then gift returns to testator's estate as a resulting trust.
Justified originally on basis that they avoid fraud on the secret beneficiary.	There never could be a fraud on the secret beneficiary – because the trust is apparent on the face of the will.
Are based on intention, communication – and operate outside the Wills Act.	Are based on intention, communication – and operate outside the Wills Act.
Could exist as either an express trust or as a constructive trust .	Can only ever operate as an express trust – because trust apparent on face of will.

Diagram illustrating the similarities and differences between fully secret trusts and half secret trusts

CHAPTER 6

PROTECTIVE AND DISCRETIONARY TRUSTS

6.1 PROTECTIVE TRUSTS

1. This is a simple device that ensures that a beneficiary who is likely to dissipate the fund through inexperience, immaturity or irresponsibility is prevented from doing so (*Re T's Settlement Trusts* (1964)).
2. It will arise where the settlor/testator knows that the trust property could be sold or mortgaged resulting in the effective waste of the assets with possible detriment to the beneficiary's spouse and children.
3. Such a trust could be drafted individually or incorporating the provisions of s33 TA 1925.
4. The beneficiary in effect receives a life interest in the property determinable in the event of, e.g. bankruptcy of the beneficiary or attempts to dispose of the assets of the trust by the beneficiary.
5. In that case a discretionary trust will usually arise.
6. Trustees can then use the property to benefit the beneficiary and his/her dependants by whatever method they select.
7. While this type of trust is useful in guarding against irresponsible use of the trust property, it can also be seen as unfair to creditors.

6.2 DISCRETIONARY TRUSTS

6.2.1 The purpose of discretionary trusts

1. By definition, a discretionary trust is one where the trustee has a power to select from a number of potential

beneficiaries to whom (s)he will distribute the assets under the trust

2. The mechanism has the advantage that beneficiaries have rights in the interest until selected – and formerly there were also specific tax saving advantages but these have now gone.

3. Discretionary trust then may be used:
   - in conjunction with protective trusts to protect the fund from beneficiaries who are irresponsible or spendthrift;
   - to protect a beneficiary against a creditor in bankruptcy;
   - to allow flexibility to take account of changing circumstances of beneficiaries.

6.2.2 How discretionary trusts operate

1. Property is normally conveyed to the trustees to be held on trust to apply either the income or the capital or both for the benefit of members of a class of beneficiaries in such proportions as the trustees in their absolute discretion think fit.

2. The trust lasts for any designated period that is not in excess of the perpetuity period, i.e. since the Perpetuities and Accumulations Act 1964 for a maximum of 80 years.

3. There may well be a power to accumulate – although this is subject to various statutory restrictions.

4. Distinction is made between 'exhaustive' discretionary trusts (where trustees are required to distribute the whole income) and 'non-exhaustive' discretionary trusts (where in relation to income the income does not have to be distributed each year, or to capital where the whole capital would not have to be distributed during the currency of the discretionary trust) (*Re Locker's Settlement* (1977)).

5. Powers may be given to add to or to exclude beneficiaries and for a resettlement on new trusts.

6.2.3 The interests of the beneficiaries

1. Unlike in fixed trusts – beneficiaries under a discretionary trust have no proprietary interest in the trust – but depend on selection by trustees.
2. If the trust is exhaustive then the class of beneficiaries as a whole if adult and not suffering any disability may terminate the trust and enforce distribution (*Re Smith* (1928)).
3. Otherwise the duty of the trustee is only to exercise the discretion.
4. In the case of a non-exhaustive discretionary trust this duty may be satisfied merely by exercising a power to accumulate.

CHAPTER 7

RESULTING TRUSTS AND CONSTRUCTIVCE TRUSTS

Constructive trusts:

Arise by operation of law – and some overlap with resulting – and basic duty is to return fund to rightful owner – but uncertain whether a trust or a remedy.

Can occur in the case of:

- Secret profit made by a fiduciary (*Boardman v Phipps*).
- Mutual wills – agreement between two parties on identity of beneficiary when both die – avoids fraud on first to die (*Re Dale*).
- Vendor of land once contract is concluded (*Lysaght v Edwards*).
- Property acquired by killing (*Re Crippen*) – subject to other rules in Forfeiture Act.
- Fully secret trusts – but not half secret (which are on face of will) – but see *Ottaway v Norman*.
- Strangers who dishonestly assist in a breach of trust (*Royal Brunei Airlines v Tan*).
- Strangers who knowingly receive trust property when it is unconscionable to do so (*Commerce International (Overseas) Ltd v Akindele*).
- Agents and partners where they act dishonestly (*Re Bell's Indenture*).
- 'New model' trusts where it is just and equitable (*Hussey v Palmer*).

Resulting trusts

Based on return of trust fund to settlor's estate:

- can be automatic (where settlor fails to dispose of entire beneficial interest);
- or presumed (from presumed intent of settlor).

Failure of express trust e.g.:

- charitable purpose not properly identified (*Re Diplock*);
- failure to meet contingency in a contingent interest (*Essery v Cowlard*).

Failure to dispose of entire beneficial interest:

- Settlor must keep what he has not disposed of (*Re Vendervell*).
- Can involve surpluses (*Re Gillingham Bus Disaster Fund*).
- Or dissolution of unincorporated associations.

Presumption in voluntary conveyance:

- Does not apply to personality (*Re Vinagradoff*).
- Can be rebutted by presumption of advancement (*Re Ekyn's*).
- Or either by evidence to contrary (*Shepard v Cartwright*).

Purchase in name of others:

- unless indication that actual purchaser does not intend to keep beneficial interest, then presumption of resulting trust in his favour (*Fowkes v Pascoe*);
- if many contributions then based on actual contribution (*Bull v Bull*).

RESULTING AND CONSTRUCTIVE TRUSTS

Trusts of the family home:

- Used as ways of dealing with implied co-ownership.
- Judges have confused implied, resulting, and constructive trusts – now re-classified in *Drake v Whipp*.
- Resulting based on implied co-owner's conribution (*Bull v Bull*).
- Constructive based on evidence of legal owner's intention to share and actual detriment suffered by implied co-owner (*Eves v Eves*).
- But constructive cannot be based on work alone (*Lloyds Bank v Rosset*).
- In many cases in 1970s CA used 'new model' constructive trust based on what was just and equitable (*Gissing v Gissing*); but HL took different view.

7.1 INTRODUCTION

1. These groups of trusts can defy simple definition because even within themselves they include many different types or arise in quite different situations.
2. The essential feature linking them all is that they are not expressly stated in a trust instrument but are implied from the circumstances in which they arise.
3. Although resulting trusts have been defined in various ways they are in essence used as the basis of an action for return of one's own property; the modern view is that they arise because of the absence of any intention by the transferor to pass any beneficial interest to the transferee.
4. Even then while some resulting trusts are implied from the presumed intention of settlor not all are – so area is far from straightforward.
5. Constructive trusts, as resulting trusts do not meet formality requirements for express trusts – but the two are still distinct.
6. The distinction is that while resulting trusts involve the real equitable owner of property asserting a continuing interest in the property, the constructive trust is imposed by the court in order to redress a breach of a fiduciary relationship.
7. It has been said that the constructive trust is a residual category which is used by the court in circumstances where it wishes to impose a trust and no other category is appropriate.
8. Extra confusion has been added at times by the application of the principles to shared ownership of domestic property.

7.2 RESULTING TRUSTS

7.2.1 General

1. A resulting trust is one that comes about through operation of law as would a constructive trust, only for different reasons.

2. In effect it occurs where a settlor retains beneficial interest in trust property – or there are indications that settlor did not intend to part with beneficial ownership of the property.

3. So often said to be based on presumed intention of settlor – though that will not always seem to be case – e.g. *Vandervell v IRC* (1967) where effect of resulting trust was to impose an extra tax burden on a settlor who was trying to avoid tax.

4. Resulting comes from the Latin 'resultare' meaning 'to spring back' – in essence, what happens to the beneficial entitlement.

5. Although it could be argued that the beneficial entitlement is actually never disposed of.

6. Resulting trusts are sometimes referred to as:
   - **presumed** – where they are said to arise from the presumed intent of the settlor;
   - **automatic** – where settlor merely fails to dispose of all of the beneficial interest.

7. There are many different situations where such trusts arise:
   - property is transferred to the trustees but the trust fails to take effect as the settlor intended it to;
   - the settlor fails to dispose of the entire interest;
   - property bought by one person but in name of another;
   - property which is already owned is transferred into the name of someone else.

7.2.2 Failure of an express trust

1. An express trust may fail for numerous reasons:
   - the settlor fails to identify the property that passes; or
   - fails to identify some or all of the beneficiaries; or
   - fails to properly identify what the interests are.

2. Or a gift may fail where a settlor fails properly to identify the specific purpose in a charitable gift –property then returns to the settlor's estate on resulting trust (*Re Diplock* (1944)).

3. If a gift fails for becoming void then again a resulting trust is created (*Re Ames' Settlement* (1946)).
4. And if any contingent requirement is not met, again, the trust fails and a resulting trust will arise (*Essery v Cowlard* (1884)).

7.2.3 Failure to dispose of the entire beneficial interest

1. Arguably most common reason why resulting trusts occur – it certainly leads to the most case law.
2. Can occur quite accidentally, e.g. as a result of poor drafting, or by a failure to provide for a particular eventuality.
3. There are four possible outcomes – not just a resulting trust:
   * if fund for charitable purposes may be redirected *cy-près*;
   * or court might construe outright gift to one beneficiary;
   * in the absence of beneficiaries on intestacy the property may be redirected to the Crown by *bona vacantia*;
   * but there may indeed be a resulting trust.
4. General rationale of applying resulting trust in such situations is argument that settlor must keep what he has not parted with – and courts must construe whether or not he has disposed of entire interest (*Vandervell v IRC* (1967)).
5. Where gifts made to specific persons for specific purposes then generally 'court always regards the gift as absolute, and the purpose merely as the motive for the gift' – (Page-Wood V-C in *Re Sanderson's Trusts* (1857)).
6. So surplus after purpose achieved may still pass absolutely to beneficiary rather than resulting trust (*Re Osoba* (1979)).
7. In rare situations, if can show that there was no intention to provide absolute benefit then resulting trust of surplus property possible (*Re Trusts of the Abbot Fund* (1900)).
8. Resulting trusts may often occur on surplus from e.g. a disaster fund (*Re Gillingham Bus Disaster Fund* (1958)).

9. Surplus funds on dissolution of unincorporated associations
   can lead to a number of possible outcomes – although in
   general what happens depends on rules of association
   which acts as a contract between the members:
   - in certain situations if a trust is accepted surplus is
     distributed amongst existing members on resulting trust
     (*Re Printers' and Transferrors' Society* (1899)).
   - although applying resulting trusts is more problematic if
     not limited to existing members (*Re Hobourn Aero
     Components Air Raid Distress Fund* (1946)).
   - if members are said to be receiving contractual benefit
     then no resulting trust (*Cunnack v Edwards* (1896)).
   - usually no resulting trust possible where fund arose
     from variety of sources not just subscriptions of
     members (*Re West Sussex Constabulary's Widows, Children
     and Benevolent (1930) Fund Trust* (1979)).
   - more modern solution is that (even if fund held on
     trust) it is distributed to members if constitution of
     association permits (*Re Bucks Constabulary Fund (No 2)*
     (1979)).
   - where entitlement is by resulting trusts then distribution
     of surplus is to all members past and present according
     to their contribution (*Re Sick and Funeral Society of St
     John's Sunday School Golcar* (1973)).

7.2.4 Voluntary conveyances and presumption of resulting trust

1. In land, prior to 1925 in order to prevent a resulting trust
   from arising in a voluntary conveyance it was necessary to
   insert an express statement that beneficial interest also
   transferred:
   - s60(3) Law of Property Act 1925 then provided that a
     resulting trust would not arise merely because an express
     statement to the contrary was not included;

- however, if an outright gift is intended then it is still best to expressly state so – to prevent a resulting trust being construed as settlor's intention *Hodgson v Marks (1971)*

2. S60(3) does not apply to pure personalty – transfer governed by general principles of equity – in voluntary transfer of personalty a resulting trust arises and transferee holds on trust for transferor (the presumption of a resulting trust) – based on idea that transferor would not wish to part with beneficial interest where there is only a voluntary transfer (although it is hard to see why they cannot be construed as outright gifts) (*Re Vinogradoff* (1935)).

3. The presumption of a resulting trust can of course be rebutted by evidence of a contrary intention – this may also be the case where the presumption of advancement applies:

   - presumption is based on relationship between settlor and beneficiary – so in certain cases outright gift presumed, e.g. husband/wife, father/children, father/any person for whom he is *in loco parentis* (*Re Ekyn's Trusts* (1877)).

   - while presumption derives from moral obligation – Lord Diplock in *Pettit v Pettit* (1970) said it is 'based upon inferences of fact which an earlier generation of judges drew as the most likely intentions of earlier generations of spouses belonging to the propertied classes of a different social era';

   - presumption will not apply to a mother's gift to her child (*Bennett v Bennett* (1879)), or a father's gift to his illegitimate child, (though in practice both should now be covered by *loco parentis*), nor to voluntary transfer from a wife to husband, or from a man to his mistress – although in all these it is suggested that more modern approach should be taken (*Re Cameron (Deceased)* (1999)).

4. Both presumptions of a resulting trust and of advancement can be rebutted by evidence to contrary – though there are

limitations on what evidence is available to rebut the presumption (*Shephard v Cartwright* (1954)).

5. Traditionally, courts were reluctant to let a party introduce evidence of an improper motive in order to rebut a presumption (*Gascoigne v Gascoigne* (1918)):
   - as Lord Denning put it in *Tinker v Tinker* (1970) it may leave the judge 'on the horns of a dilemma';
   - the whole area of improper motive was reviewed by both CA and HL – with HL determining that interests under illegal transactions can be enforced only if the party seeking to can establish their title without relying on their own illegality – and rejecting CA's idea that the answer should be based on what does or does not offend public conscience (*Tinsley v Milligan* (1993));
   - one further point established is that presumption of advancement can be rebutted by evidence of unlawful or improper motive when purpose not actually carried out – the so-called 'repentance' principle (*Tribe v Tribe* (1996)).
   - the Law Commission has been critical of courts' handling of these issues and has suggested reforms.

7.2.5 Purchase in the name of others and the presumption of resulting trust

1. As Chief Baron Eyre said in *Dyer v Dyer* (1788) 'the trust of a legal estate ... results to the man who advances the purchase money'.
2. So whenever a person has bought property in another's name, unless there is some indication that he does not intend to keep beneficial interest, there is a presumption of a resulting trust in his favour (*Fowkes v Pascoe* (1875)).
3. As with voluntary transfers of property, the presumption of advancement can rebut the presumption of a resulting trust and the same rules apply as to admissibility of evidence (*Warren v Gurney* (1944)).

4. Where purchase by several parties is made in name of one then title held on resulting trust in proportion to which each contributed to purchase – and this is particularly appropriate to implied co-ownership cases – *Bull v Bull* (1955) and *Pettit v Pettit* (1970) and *Gissing v Gissing* (1971) – and criticisms of earlier cases were aired and precise difference between application of resulting trust and constructive trust was identified in *Drake v Whipp* (1995).

5. If a joint purchase is put in name of one person who is wife or child of the other party then presumption of advancement arises in any case as a last resort and can be rebutted by very comparatively slight evidence (*McGrath v Wallis* (1995)).

6. Law Commission has been critical and suggested reforms.

7.3 CONSTRUCTIVE TRUSTS

7.3.1 General

1. A constructive trust is a form of implied trust which arises only by operation of law.

2. According to Edmund Davies LJ in *Carl Zeiss Stiftung v Herbert Smith & Co* (1969) 'English law provides no clear and all-embracing definition… Its boundaries have been left perhaps deliberately vague, so as not to restrict the court by technicalities in deciding what the justice of a particular case may demand'.

3. However, the mechanism has been crucial to the development of real property rights in English law.

4. There are certain overlaps with resulting trusts, e.g. that neither conform to the formality requirements, but, though they have been, the two should not be confused.

5. Another major questions to follow the constructive trust is whether it exists as a type of trust or is in fact a remedy.

7.3.2 Duties of the constructive trustee

1. Duties and liabilities of a constructive trustee are generally different to those of an express trustee.
2. This is because the trusts arises by operation of law.
3. So, e.g. duties to invest and general duty of care will not apply.
4. And duties will probably vary according to circumstances in which the trusts arises.
5. Certainly in many instances the most significant duty of the constructive trustee will be to return the property (or to account for it) to the actual beneficiary.
6. This is why in certain jurisdictions, e.g. USA, the trust is seen as being essentially remedial, has to do with restitution, and is a means of preventing unjust enrichment.
7. Although the English courts have generally tended to reject this approach – e.g. in the case of mortgage arrears *Halifax Building Society v Thomas* (1996) and in the case of the assets of an insolvent company (*Re Polly Peck International plc (in administration) (No 2)* (1998)).

7.3.3 Traditional categories of constructive trust

1. Where a fiduciary obtains an unauthorised (secret) profit as a result of his/her connection with the trust:
   - the basic principle is that from Lord Herschell's judgment in *Bray v Ford* (1896) 'a person in a fiduciary position ... is not, unless otherwise expressly provided, entitled to make a profit; he is not allowed to put himself in a position where his interest and his duty conflict';
   - and the fiduciary will be prevented from keeping any advantage gained directly or indirectly from the position as fiduciary (*Re Biss* (1903)).

- And in such circumstances fiduciary holds property gained on constructive trust for beneficiaries under the trust (*Boardman v Phipps* (1967)).

2. Mutual wills:
   - where two people, usually husband and wife, leave property to each other, but also agree that on the death of survivor of two property should go to named beneficiaries;
   - there must be a clear and binding agreement between the parties not to revoke the will – compare *Re Oldham* (1925) with *Re Cleaver* (1981);
   - to maintain rule that wills should always be revocable but still allow agreement to be enforceable, equity imposes a trust on personal representatives of second of two parties to agreement to die in favour of ultimate beneficiary identified in agreement (*Dufour v Pereira* (1769));
   - one argument used to justify enforcing mutual will is that survivor of two parties to agreement is receiving some benefit – and it is this that makes it inequitable for that party to go back on the agreement;
   - disputed by Morritt J in *Re Dale (Deceased)* (1994) – where it was stated that the theoretical basis of the trust is to prevent fraud against the other party to an agreement that was intended by both to be binding;
   - it is likely that the trust arises on the death of the first party – but there are then difficulties in determining to what property the trust applies (*Re Hagger* (1930));
   - area is full of difficulties and has been said 'is a clumsy and inadequate way of dealing with a complicated problem' (Martin).

3. The vendor of land:
   - not an ordinary trusteeship – because a contract for land is specifically enforceable – once contract is concluded purchaser becomes effective owner of land and vendor in that sense is trustee of it (*Lysaght v Edwards* (1876));

- uncertain at which precise point vendor becomes trustee;
- but it is possible that where after exchange of contracts vendor then sells on to a different purchaser (s)he may be constructive trustee of the purchase monies for benefit of purchaser (*Lake v Bayliss* (1974));
- on completion once the price is paid property must be conveyed because at this stage vendor has only a bare legal estate while purchaser owns entire beneficial interest (*Lloyds Bank plc v Carrick* (1996));
- this is an example of the maxim that equity treats as done that which ought to be done.

4. Acquisition of property by killing:
   - English courts have established rules to ensure that beneficiaries who kill the testator (or someone they would inherit from in intestacy) should not profit from the killing (*Re Crippen* (1911));
   - in certain circumstances the killer is said to hold on a constructive trust for the person who would be next entitled under the deceased's will or by intestacy rules;
   - but the area is not without difficulty and is complicated, e.g. by the Forfeiture Act 1982.

5. Secret trusts:
   - there is debate as to whether secret trusts are constructive trusts or express trusts;
   - half secret trusts can only ever be express because the trust is clear in the will;
   - but with fully secret, if they operate to prevent fraud by the ostensible beneficiary they could be constructive;
   - the significance is that for express trusts of land s53(1)(b) Law of Property Act 1925 must be complied with but not in a constructive trust;
   - in *Ottaway v Norman* an oral fully secret trust of land was upheld without the issue being discussed.

7.3.4 Constructive trusts involving strangers to the trust

1. Strangers to the trust are people who are not themselves express trustees but intermeddle in the trust:
   - they may be made personally liable for their dishonest involvement in a breach of trust; or
   - they may come into possession of trust property and then be obliged to hold it on trust for the beneficiaries.
2. Dishonest assistance:
   - now more correctly described as 'accessory liability'
   - on the basis of Lord Selborne's judgment in *Barnes v Addy* (1874) it was originally taken that the accessory was not liable unless the breach of trust arose from the dishonesty of the trustee;
   - now it is accepted that it is the accessory's dishonesty that is critical regardless of whether the trustee has been dishonest – otherwise the accessory could get away with unconscionable behaviour merely because the trustee acted honestly (*Royal Brunei Airlines v Tan* (1995));
   - on this basis the liability of the accessory is really personal but it has been suggested that using the label of constructive trust is to avoid the difficulty of a beneficiary not being able to sue anybody but a trustee;
   - where an accessory is not dishonest and there is a breach of trust still then the action is against the trustees (*Lipkin Gorman v Karpnale Ltd* (1989)).
3. Knowing receipt and dealing:
   - now more appropriately called 'recipient liability';
   - a person in actual receipt of trust property has always been bound to return the property unless (s)he is a *bona fide* purchaser for value without notice – and so long as (s)he retains the property tracing is possible;
   - formerly, constructive notice was sufficient for the person in the receipt of the property to take subject to the trust (*Belmont Finance Corporation v Williams Furniture Ltd (No 2)* (1980));

- however, a different view was taken by Megarry V-C in *Re Montagu's Settlement Trusts* (1987) – where it was suggested that only actual knowledge is sufficient;
- reviewing the authorities Nourse LJ in *Bank of Credit and Commerce International (Overseas) Ltd v Akindele* (2000) considered that for recipient liability 'The recipient's state of knowledge must be such as to make it unconscionable for him to retain the benefit of the receipt' – although accepting that this strict liability may be inappropriate to commercial transactions.

4. An agent who knowingly receives trust property will not be liable 'so long as he acts honestly ... unless he intermeddles in the trust by doing acts ... outside the duties of an agent' *Williams – Ashman v Price and Williams* (1942).

5. Liability of partners of a constructive trustee:
   - since partners are jointly and severally liable a partner may be equally liable for his partner's misapplication of trust monies;
   - but this will not be the case where the partner has acted honestly throughout and has not received funds as a trustee but only as an agent (*Re Bell's Indenture* (1980));
   - in *Blyth v Fladgate* (1891) solicitors who were partners became trustees because there were no trustees at the time that the money was paid into their account;
   - but it has also been held that a partnership can be vicariously liable under s10 Partnership Act 1890 for torts and also as constructive trustee (*Dubai Aluminum v Salaam* (1998)).

7.3.5 The 'new model' constructive trusts

1. Term 'new model' adopted by Denning in *Eves v Eves* (1975).
2. He felt that such trusts should be applied wherever 'just and reasonable' regardless of rules (*Hussey v Palmer* (1972)).

3. So applied by Lord Denning in cases involving share of family home (spouses or cohabitees) based on work done etc (*Gissing v Gissing* (1971); *Eves v Eves; Petit v Petit* (1970)).

4. But the common feature was that the party would have failed under traditional trust or land law principles.

5. So HL often took different line to CA (*Gissing v Gissing*).

6. And recent decisions have avoided this application (*Lloyds Bank plc v Rossett (1991); Drake v Whipp* (1996)).

7. Although apparent variations of 'new model' trusts have been used in avoiding the restrictions of registered land in *Peffer v Rigg* (1977) and *Lyus v Prowsa Developments Ltd* (1982)).

8. The 'new model' actually goes well beyond being remedial and acts to prevent the trustee's unjust enrichment.

7.4 TRUSTS OF THE FAMILY HOME

7.4.1 The nature of implied co-ownership

1. Whenever land is conveyed to two or more people they are both entitled as beneficial as well as legal owners – express co-ownership.

2. Implied co-ownership is also possible – often where there is only one legal owner (i.e. the grant or conveyance is in a single name but circumstances show that there is an additional owner(s) of the beneficial interest, e.g. where a wife contributes towards purchase of matrimonial home.

3. In implied co-ownership the legal owner now holds on a trust of land (but formerly on a trust for sale) the beneficial title for himself and all other beneficial owners.

4. Certain problems are created by this situation:
   - with only one legal title holder, there is only one trustee creating complications for the overreaching mechanism in land transfers;

- the problem of protecting the beneficial owner's interest, particularly rights of occupation;
- disputes over sales of the property.

5. There are generally two ways in which the beneficial interest can arise to become an implied co-ownership:
   - where there is a resulting trust – requiring a contribution to the acquisition of the property;
   - where there is a constructive trust – based on a presumed agreement of the parties that the implied co-owner is to own a beneficial share.

6. Sometimes judges have confused constructive and resulting trusts, or suggested the distinction is unimportant, or have referred to implied trusts as a separate category to the other two, and Lord Denning made it even more complex in certain cases – but since *Drake v Whipp* (1995) the classification above is probably the most accurate.

7.4.2 Implied co-ownership under a resulting trust

1. The basis of the resulting trust is that the person claiming implied co-ownership has made a contribution towards the acquisition of the property.

2. The resulting trust has many applications in diverse areas of law, e.g. company law – a traditional example of a resulting trust in land ownership is where a person made a grant of property with an express trust which failed to dispose of the whole beneficial interest, then trustees would hold the residue on a resulting trust for the settlor.

3. The obvious example of a resulting trust is where two or more people jointly contribute (in whatever proportions) to the purchase of land but the legal estate is in one name only – the legal owner holds on resulting trust for both his/her own and the other party's beneficial interest (*Bull v Bull* (1955)).

4. And such trusts frequently occur in relation to matrimonial homes (*Kingsnorth Trust Co. Ltd. v Tizard* (1986)).

5. Another classic example is a bare trust where the conveyance of legal title was to a 'volunteer' who gave no consideration, unless it can be shown that the property was transferred as a gift (*Hodgson v Marks* (1971)).

6. Where there is a gift of land no trust exists – the whole beneficial ownership is transferred (*Tinsley v Milligan* (1992)).

7. A presumption of trust is rebuttable by raising the presumption of advancement – that a gift is made in specific relationships e.g. father and daughter where one is bound to materially support the other (*Stock v McAvoy* (1872)).

8. In family law, 'property adjustment orders' may now give entitlement in land to spouses on divorce – first introduced in Matrimonial Proceedings and Property Act 1970, and now contained in Matrimonial Causes Act 1973, as amended by Family Law Act 1996 – clearly, before these provisions were introduced, the need to prove a trust was greater.

9. In cohabitation cases this is still be necessary as provisions only apply to married couples (*Windeler v Whitehall* (1990)).

10. Direct financial contribution to purchase of property creates a resulting trust straightforwardly in favour of contributor (so a contribution to mortgage repayments is equally acceptable as a contribution to a deposit or a cash purchase) – but contributions in another form are more problematic – the point being that it is often vital to prove them to protect one party's right to continued occupation of the family home.

11. So the courts have had to consider claims based on minor contributions to household expenses and work done – accepted as creating a resulting trust by the Court of Appeal but rejected by the House of Lords (*Pettit v Pettit* (1970)).

12. And purchase of necessary household equipment (*Gissing v Gissing* (1971)) – again accepted in CA but rejected in HL.

13. And it is possible that a contribution to regular domestic expenses may create an interest but only where it is only by this that the legal owner can actually make the purchase.

14. Sometimes court confuses law by not distinguishing between resulting and constructive trusts (*Hussey v Palmer* (1972)).

15. This confusion created by the courts was specifically criticised in *Drake v Whipp* (1995) and the distinction between the two types of trust re-emphasised.

16. So share under resulting trust is directly proportional to contribution.

7.4.3 Implied co-ownership under a constructive trust

1. A constructive trust arises by operation of law and is imposed on owner of legal title usually as result of his conduct.

2. So may be imposed as result of fraudulent, unconscionable, or inequitable conduct on part of the legal title holder.

3. There are essentially three elements:
   - a common intention expressed by the parties (not necessarily in writing);
   - reliance on this promise made by legal title owner by party claiming an interest evidenced by sufferance of some detriment on their part;
   - unconscionable behaviour by legal title owner.

4. So first job for court is to identify a common intention:
   - which may arise from the simple promise of title holder (*Eves v Eves* (1975));
   - or where title holder has negatively explained the reason that the beneficial owner is excluded from the title (*Grant v Edwards [1986]* or *Hammond v Mitchell* (1991)).

5. Features identifiable as a detriment have included financial expenditure, e.g. household expenses (*Hazell v Hazell* (1972)).

6. Although generally a stricter line has been taken by the courts (*Burns v Burns* (1983)).

7. More recently a claim to a constructive trust based on work alone has failed (*Lloyds Bank v Rosset* (1991)).

8. In any case neither payment of household expenses nor work done is sufficient where it is the express intention of the title holder that the beneficial ownership should not be shared (*Thomas v Fuller-Brown* (1988)).

9. Unconscionable behaviour arises where it can be shown that a purchase that was made on an oral agreement to share was not reduced to writing in order to retain outright ownership (*Bannister v Bannister* (1948)).

10. And a constructive trust can be imposed where a written agreement fails to accurately represent the oral agreement and therefore is based on inequitable or fraudulent behaviour in securing it (*Binions v Evans* (1972)).

7.4.4 The 'fair and equitable' cases

1. Distinctions between resulting trusts and constructive trusts of land identified by HL in *Gissing v Gissing* is quite precise but judgment is confusing as it refers to three types of trust.

2. Immediate consequence of HL judgment was that CA, and in particular Lord Denning, made increased use of non-express trusts to achieve a fair result where strict application of legal rules would act inequitably to the party claiming beneficial entitlement – these are known as the 'fair and equitable' cases, and they are inconsistent with the general principles.

3. They were granted when:
    • work done on the house represented a constructive trust on behalf of a woman cohabitee (*Cooke v Head* (1972));

- a small contribution made to build extension to accommodate an elderly in-law, and, in absence of any obvious agreement to share a constructive trust used to rebut the presumption of a gift (*Hussey v Palmer* (1972));
- it would be inequitable to deny an interest because of work done and care shown to the cohabitee and children (*Eves v Eves* (1975));
- contributions towards household expenses in cohabitation represented a contribution sufficient to imply a trust (*Hall v Hall* (1982)).

4. *Pettit v Pettit* and *Gissing v Gissing* were also decided on 'fair and equitable' principles by CA but reversed by HL.

5. CA in *Drake v Whipp* expressed dissatisfaction with the cavalier approach taken to choice of trust in cases such as *Hussey v Palmer* and described earlier judicial statements on implied co-ownership as 'a potent source of confusion'.

6. Judgments of CA in *Burns v Burns* and HL in *Lloyds Bank v Rosset* have stuck more to restrictive distinctions identified by HL in *Gissing v Gissing* and it is unlikely that attitudes of Lord Denning and CA in 1970's will be followed.

CHAPTER 8

CHARITABLE TRUSTS

Charitable objects
Must conform to 'spirit and intendment' of preamble to 1601 statute.

Now MacNaghten's four categories from *IRC v Pemsell* – subject to Lord Wilberforce's requirement in *Scottish Burial* case that charity is not a fixed concept and to be found by analogy with case law:
Relief of poverty:
● no general definition – but not destitution (*Re Coulthurst*);
● includes widows and orphans (*Re Young*), and distressed gentlefolk (*Thompson v Thompson*);
● not working class (*Re Sander's W T*);
● nor if rich can receive (*Re Gwyon*);
● can include poor relatives (*Re Scarisbrick*);
● and poor employees (*Dingle v Turner*).

Advancement of education:
● includes any form of worthwhile instruction or cultural pursuit (*Incorporated Council of Law Reporting v A-G for England & Wales*);
● and useful research – compare (*Re Hopkins* and *Re Shaw*);
● and aesthetics, e.g. literature (*Re Hopkins*), music (*Re Delius*);
● but must have value (*Re Pinion*);
● and sport (*IRC v McMullen*);
● politics more difficult – compare *Re Koepplers* and *Re Hopkinson*.
Advancement of religion:
● requires supernatural being plus related code of behaviour;
● but not ethics alone (*Re Southplace Ethical Society*);
● and needs public involvement – compare *Re Hetherington* and *Gilmour v Coates*.
Other purposes beneficial to the community:
● includes trusts for animal welfare (*Re Wedgwood*);
● and recreation (*Re Gray*);
● but difficulties in *IRC v Baddeley* led to Recreational Charites Act;
● trusts for old and disable (*Rowntree Housing Association v A-G*);
● miscellaneous, e.g. hospitals (*Re Resch*).

Public benefit:
● Different for each head.
● Generally presumed in relief of poverty depending on size of class (*Re Scarisbrick*).
● More difficult to find in education – test in *Oppenheim v Tobacco Securities Trust Securities* – (i) class not numerically negligible; (ii) distinguishing feature not dependent on individual.
● In religious trusts depends on public access compare *Re Hetherington* and *Gilmour v Coates*.
● 4th head test is between relief extended to whole community but advantaged only to few and form select few from large number (*IRC v Baddeley*).

CHARITABLE TRUSTS

Wholly and exclusively charitable:
● Usually political motive fails (*McGovern v A-G*).
● Gift succeeds if other purposes are only ancillary (*Re Coxen*).
● Problems if trust drafted too widely (*IRC v Baddeley*).
● Or if linked to other purposes by disjunctive words (*Chichester Diocesan Fund and Board of Finance Ltd v Simpson*).
● More likely to succeed with conjunctives link words, e.g. *Re Sutton* 'charitable and deserving' and *Re Best* 'charitable and benevolent'.
● Can save by severance or Charitable Trusts (Validation) Act.

8.1 THE HISTORY OF THE CHARITABLE TRUST

1. Medieval society upheld charitable gifts wherever possible – pre-eminence of religion – benefit to church – but disliked by Parliament – 'mortmain' (inalienability).

2. Changed by reformation and seizure of church lands – loss of charitable activities carried out by church – so burden on parish – or disorder resulted.

3. Parliament changed attitudes with Statute of Charitable Uses 1601 (the Elizabethan statute) – commissioners appointed to oversee administration of charitable gifts

4. Preamble defined charitable: 'relief of aged, impotent, and poor people; maintenance of sick and maimed soldiers and mariners; schools of learning, free schools, and scholars in universities; repair of bridges, ports, havens, causeways, churches, seabanks and highways; education and preferment of orphans; the relief, stock or maintenance of houses of correction; marriage of poor maids; supportation, aid, and help of young tradesmen, handicraftsmen, and persons decayed; the relief or redemption of prisoners or captives; the aid or ease of any poor inhabitants concerning the payment of fifteens, setting out of soldiers, and other taxes'.

5. Subsequent statutory intervention:
   - 1601 statute, repealed in Mortmain and Charitable Uses Act 1888 – but expressly preserved preamble;
   - Charities Act 1960 – preamble repealed in s38(4);
   - Charities Act 1993 – repealed 1960 Act preserved s38(4).

6. So 'spirit and intendment' preserved in case law. Lord MacNaghten in *Commissioners of IRC v Pemsell* – 'no doubt the popular meaning of the words 'charity' and 'charitable' does not coincide with their legal meaning … 'charity' in its legal sense comprises four principal divisions: trusts for the relief of poverty; trusts for the advancement of

education; trusts for the advancement of religion; and trusts for other purposes beneficial to the community, not … under any of the preceding heads'.

7. *Scottish Burial Reform and Crematorium Society v Glasgow Corporation* (1968) – Lord Wilberforce: 'It is now accepted that what must be regarded as charitable is not the wording of the preamble itself, but the effect of the decisions given by the court as to its scope … which have endeavoured to keep the law … moving according as new social need arises or old ones become obsolete and satisfied'.

8. So can use appropriate wording but gift fails because real purpose not charitable (*McGovern v A-G* (1982)).

8.2 THE DIFFERENCE BETWEEN CHARITABLE TRUSTS AND OTHER TRUSTS

1. Private trusts benefit individuals – charitable benefit society in general as well as individuals.
2. Charitable trusts for purposes so no human beneficiaries.
3. There is no requirement for certainty.
4. Charitable trusts may be perpetual.
5. They also gain significant tax exemptions:
   - income tax – s505 Income and Corporation Tax Act 1988;
   - exempt from capital gains tax and inheritance tax;
   - also from stamp duty on conveyancing;
   - and from national insurance surcharge;
   - and also 80% exemption from non-domestic rates;
   - in 1997 tax exemption amounted to £1.75 billion – so not surprising so many cases brought by IRC.

8.3 ESSENTIAL REQUIREMENTS OF CHARITABLE TRUSTS

1. For gift to be charitable there are three principal requirements:
   - gift must be for purpose which falls 'within the spirit and intendment' of preamble to Statute of Elizabeth;
   - trust must promote public benefit accepted by courts;
   - purposes must be wholly and exclusively charitable.
2. What is charitable is a question of law, not settlor's intentions.
3. First of three above tests is tested against categories identified in Lord MacNaghten's judgment in *Pemsell*:
   - trusts for the relief of poverty;
   - trusts for the advancement of education;
   - trusts for the advancement of religion;
   - trusts for other purposes beneficial to community.
3. Subject to *Scottish Burial* case point – social needs and attitudes change – so that list is not exhaustive.

8.4 CHARITABLE OBJECTS

8.4.1 Trusts for the relief of poverty

1. Poverty is not generally defined – but it need not mean destitution (*Re Coulthurst* (1951)).
2. Poverty in any case is a shifting concept over time – and in many ways has been superseded by the welfare state.
3. Need not be for poor – *A-G v Power* (1809) widows and orphans; *Re Young* (1951) distressed gentlefolk; *Thompson v Thompson* (1844) unsuccessful writers.
4. 'Working class' need not be poor; compare *Re Sanders' Will Trusts* (1954) and *Re Niyazi's Will Trusts* (1978).
5. So failure to avoid wealthy recipients will cause a gift to fail (*Re Gwyon* (1930)).
6. Gift to poor relations upheld in *Re Scarisbrick* (1951).

7. And for poor employees in *Dingle v Turner* (1972).
8. Trusts for poverty succeed whenever presumed to benefit people in need (*Biscoe v Jackson* (1887)).
9. They more easily satisfy the public benefit requirement.

8.4.2 Trusts for the advancement of education

1. Described in preamble as 'maintenance of schools of learning, free schools, and scholars in universities'.
2. Modern cases have widened to include 'any form of worthwhile instruction or cultural advancement except for purely professional courses' (*Incorporated Council of Law Reporting for England & Wales v A-G* (1972)).
3. Originally gift often valid when attached to educational institution (*Re Shaw's Will Trust* (1952)).
4. But if primary purpose of institution is profit making, gift may fail (*Re Girls' Public Day School Trust* (1951)).
5. Professional bodies not usually seen as charitable but can be if charitable purpose identified *Royal College of Surgeons of England v National Provincial Bank Ltd (1952)*
6. Research can be charitable because can benefit public:
   - so must be of educational value to researcher or add to store of public knowledge (*Re Hopkins' Will Trust* (1965));
   - but must involve useful knowledge (*Re Shaw* (1957)).
7. Courts will also accept art and aesthetics as charitable (*Royal Choral Society v IRC* (1943)) including:
   - music (*Re Delius* (1957));
   - artefacts and antiquities (*Re British School of Egyptian Archaeology* (1954));
   - literature (*Re Hopkins' Will Trusts* (1965));
   - but if no artistic merit gift will fail (*Re Pinion* (1965)).
8. Sport and recreation attached to educational institutions:
   - may succeed where it benefits young people but fail otherwise (*Re Mariette* (1915));
   - And facilities need not be restricted to particular school or university (*IRC v McMullen* (1981));

- but gifts for bodies outside of education will usually fail
  (*Re Nottage (1895)* and *Re Clifford* (1912));
- courts impose limits to avoid – 'a slippery slope from
  chess to draughts to bridge to whist to stamp collecting
  to acquiring birds' eggs' (*Re Dupree's Deed Trusts*
  (1945)).
9. Question of political educational is much more confused:
   - generally, political purposes are not charitable (*Re
     Hopkinson* (1949));
   - though gifts with political objects can succeed if not
     party political (*Re Koeppler's Will Trusts* (1986));
   - contradict by some cases (*Re Scowcroft* (1898));
   - where a body attached to education is identifiably
     charitable it may still be prevented from using funds for
     political purposes (*Baldry v Feintuck* (1972)).

8.4.3 Trusts for the advancement of religion

1. Reference in preamble merely to 'repair of churches'.
2. Modern definition of religion has developed – and
   numerous 'sects' have benefited from charitable status.
3. Originally meaning of religion quite narrow – but change
   to a multi-cultural society has meant a wider meaning must
   be adopted (*Bowman v Secular Society* (1917)).
4. Relationship between religion and charity tested against
   two criteria and five indicia (*Church of the New Faith v
   Commissioners of the Payroll Tax (Victoria)* (1982)).
   Criteria:
   - a belief in a supernatural being;
   - acceptance of code of behaviour to effect belief.
   Indicia:
   - collection of ideas involves belief in the supernatural,
     i.e. beyond the senses;
   - ideas relate to man's nature and place in universe;
   - ideas are accepted by adherents as requiring conforming
     to a code of behaviour;

- adherents form identifiable group, even if disparate;
- adherents see their ideas and practices as religion.

5. So ethics alone will not be religion (*Re South Place Ethical Society* (1980)).
6. Bodies with similar objectives to religions may still be classed as not charitable (*Keren Kayemeth Le Jisroel v IRC* (1931)).
7. And merely requiring belief in God will not make a body charitable (*United Grand Lodge of Ancient Free and Accepted Masons v Holborn Borough Council* (1957)).
8. Advancement requires public involvement – compare *Holmes v A-G* (1981) with *Gilmour v Coates* (1949).
9. Gifts for related purposes can be upheld (*Re King* (1923)).
10. Gifts to non-standard Christian groups upheld (*Re Manser* (1905) and *Re Strickland's Will Trusts* (1936)).
11. Also to non-Christian religions (*Varsani v Jesovani* (1999)).
12. But courts are conscious that it is an area that can be subject to 'crankish views' (*Thornton v Howe* (1862)).
13. If the gift is 'for God's work' or at discretion of clergy, wording is vital – compare *Farley v Westminster Bank* (1939), *Re Eastes* (1948) and *Re Stratton* (1931).

8.4.4 Other purposes beneficial to the community

1. Residual head – public benefit being critical.
2. Follows from preamble – so new categories developed by analogy to preamble and subsequent case law.
3. And public benefit must be in a way that is recognised as charitable (*Williams' Trustees v IRC* (1947)).
4. Gift may fail for political character (*Re Strakosch* (1949)).
5. Whether gift is of public benefit is measured objectively (*National Anti-Vivisection Society v IRC* (1948)).
6. Modern method is to identify if any reasons for not upholding gift (*Incorporated Council of Law Reporting v A-G* (1972)).

7. Major categories accepted by the courts include:
- trusts for animals:
  - improving man's humanity (*Re Wedgwood* (1915));
  - so animal welfare can be charitable (*Re Moss* (1949));
  - but not if public excluded (*Re Grove-Grady* (1929)).
- trusts for sporting and recreational facilities:
  - sport alone is not charitable (*Re Nottage* (1895));
  - but can be if for advancement of education (*IRC v McMullen* (1981));
  - and can be charitable if incidental to provision of education (*Re Gray* (1925));
  - but wording of gift is critical (*IRC v City of Glasgow Police Athletics Association* (1950));
  - and inclusion of purely social purposes may cause gift to fail (*IRC v Baddeley* (1955));
  - the case cast doubt on many charitable institutions – so led to Recreational Charities Act 1958.
- the Recreational Charities Act 1958 was passed to ensure charitable status for boys clubs, womens' institutes, the National Playing Fields Association, and other bodies affected potentially by *Baddeley* – but possibly creates as many problems as it solves:
  - s1(1) says charitable status shall be presumed for recreational facilities that are provided in interest of welfare and public benefit is evident;
  - s1(2) defines social welfare:
    - (a) facilities improve condition of life of those persons for whom they are provided;
    - (b) (i) those persons need facility because of age, youth or infirmity; or
      - (ii) they are available to public generally;
  - s1(3) applies s1(1) particularly to village halls, community centres, women's' institutes;
  - but Act appears to have little effect on cases such as *Williams* and *Baddeley*;

- although a gift with object of promoting physical well being of public in general has succeeded (*Guild v IRC* (1992)).
- trusts for old and disabled:
  - in preamble, poverty referred to as 'aged, impotent, and poor' – three categories can be seen disjunctively (*Re Robinson* (1951));
  - no precise age (*Re Cottam's Will Trusts* (1955));
  - gift might stand even though aged person can profit from it (*Rowntree Housing Association v A-G* (1983));
  - 'impotent' referred to disability (*Re Lewis* (1955)).
- miscellaneous trusts beneficial to the community:
  - gift to RNLI (*Thomas v Howell* (1874));
  - gift to museum (*British Museum v White* (1826));
  - hospital/medical facilities (*Re Resch's Will Trusts* (1969)).

8.5 THE POLITICAL ELEMENT

1. Usually, political purposes are not charitable (*Re Bushnell* (1975)).
2. Reasons to deny charitable status include: no means of ensuring that change in law would benefit public; court must decide in light of current law; court might be seen as not acting impartially (*McGovern v A-G* (1982)).
3. But there is apparent inconsistency in approach – compare *Re Koeppler* and *Re Scowcroft*.
4. Charity Commission has given revised guidelines.

8.6 THE PUBLIC BENEFIT ELEMENT

1. All charitable gifts have different public benefit requirements and relief of poverty is simpler to show.

2. Here public benefit is presumed but a key issue is how narrow class benefited can be for gift still to survive – see *Re Scarisbrick* and *Dingle v Turner*.

3. In educational trusts, public benefit more difficult to find:
   - must distinguish between personal (not charitable) and impersonal relationships (charitable) (*Re Compton* (1945));
   - test is now that (i) class is not numerically negligible; and (ii) quality that distinguishes them from rest of community does not depend on relationship with a specific individual (*Oppenheim v Tobacco Securities Trust Co* (1951));
   - a further problem is determining what is and is not a personal relationship (*Dingle v Turner* (1972)).

4. In religious trusts, public benefit problem is usually whether or not public have access – compare *Gilmour v Coates* with *Re Hetherington Deceased* (1989).

5. With final head, public benefit is particularly important:
   - a distinction has been drawn between a gift for a section of the public and a gift for 'a fluctuating body of private individuals' (*Verge v Somerville* (1924));
   - but has been argued against in *Dingle v Turner*;
   - better test is between 'a form of relief extended to the whole community yet by its very nature advantaged only to a few and a form of relief accorded to a select few out of a large number equally willing to take advantage of it' (*IRC v Baddeley* (1955)).

8.7 EXCLUSIVITY OF CHARITABLE OBJECTS

1. Trust may be invalid if for other than charitable purposes – and similarly can be invalid if charitable part cannot be separated from other purposes.

2. If other purposes merely subsidiary to main charitable purpose, then gift may succeed (*Re Coxen* (1948)).

3. Mere fact that another person benefits will not defeat it (*London Hospital Medical College v IRC* (1976)).

4. And motive of donor is irrelevant (*Re King* (1923)).

5. But problems can arise where trust drafted too widely (*McGovern v A-G* (1982) and *IRC v Baddeley* (1955)).

6. One further problem occurs where word 'charitable' linked with other words in gift – to succeed, these may need to be linked by disjunctive rather than conjunctive words (*Chichester Diocesan Fund and Board of Finance Ltd v Simpson* (1944)):

   - If disjunctive words used, question of construction whether gift succeeds – compare *Blair v Duncan* (1902) with *Re Bennett* (1920) (disjunctive words succeed because of use of 'other objects' throughout – meaning that by *ejusdem generis* the 'or' was not actually disjunctive);

   - with conjunctive words, gift more likely to succeed – *Re Sutton* (1885): 'charitable and deserving' and *Re Best* (1904): 'charitable and benevolent';

   - though this is not always possible (*A-G of the Bahamas v Royal Trust Co* (1986));

   - gift may fail if extra words used (*Re Eades* (1920));

   - again, because other words can be seen as other than charitable – so again construction is vital (*A-G v National Provincial Bank of England* (1924)).

7. There are two potential ways round the problem:

   - doctrine of severance (*Salusbury v Denton* (1857)) – remove offending words on construction

   - the Charitable Trusts (Validation) Act 1954 – read the gift as being only for charitable purposes.

8.8 THE BASIS OF THE *CY-PRÈS* DOCTRINE AT COMMON LAW

1. Ancient doctrine designed to save charitable gifts that fail for whatever reason.
2. Usual effect of failure would be a resulting trust, which may be against the settlor's express wishes – so *cy-près* tries to ensure gift redirected to similar charitable purpose if possible
3. Before Charities Act 1960, doctrine was narrow and only applied if gift failed for impossibility or impracticability – but reformed in ss13 and 14 which moved away from such rigidity.
4. The widest example of common law was *Re Dominion Students' Hall Trust* (1947).
5. Where *cy-près* applies, distinction drawn between initial failure and subsequent failure – latter easier as gift already vested.

8.9 INITIAL FAILURE

1. If gift cannot take effect on date of gift, e.g. because body that is object of gift no longer exists, there are two possibilities:
   - the gift fails and falls into residue;
   - the property can be reapplied *cy-près*.
2. Court must find wider charitable intent (*Re Rymer* (1895)).
3. So if intent of donor is wide enough to include general charitable intent then gift may succeed (*Re Lysaght* (1966)).
4. And this will often be because of impossible or impracticable conditions imposed in gift (*Re Woodham Deceased* (1981)).
5. And a gift that fails because a project cannot be carried out can still be rescued by *cy-près* (*Re Wilson* (1913)).

6. A gift to a specific charity will not fail because it has ceased if it is shown to continue in another form (*Re Faraker* (1912)).

7. But if a gift is to a named body, distinction is drawn between unincorporated associations and charitable corporations – a gift to an unincorporated charity must be charitable because no individual can identify a claim to a share – where a gift to a corporation is a gift simply to the corporation in its own name (*Re Vernon's Will Trusts* (1972)).
   - so a gift to a defunct charitable corporation fails and falls into residue and *cy-près* possible only if wider charitable intent can be found (*Re Finger's Will Trusts* (1972));
   - possible conflict of reasoning in *Faraker* and *Vernon's*.

8. If a gift is made to a body that has never existed it is said to be easier to apply *cy-près* than one to a body that has ceased to exist (*Re Harwood* (1936)).

9. If a settlor makes a number of gifts all that are charitable except one then it may be possible to see a general charitable intent (*Re Satterthwaite's Will Trusts* (1966)).

10. But if disputed part of gift is to known non-charitable body, no *cy-près* and gift falls into residue (*Re Jenkins' Will Trusts* (1966)).

8.10 SUBSEQUENT FAILURE

1. If gift fails after it is vested then no lapse of gift and no need to find a wider charitable intent (*Re Wright* (1954)).

2. This is because the property has transferred at the moment of the settlor's death – so *cy-près* can apply (*Re Slevin* (1891)).

3. But less consistency where failure is because of surplus fund – compare *Re King* (1923) with *Re Standford* (1924).

8.11 NON-CHARITABLE ALTERNATIVES

1. Settlor can decide what is to be done in event of a failure – which of course may be charitable or non-charitable.
2. So in an *inter vivos* gift failed gift might return to settlor, or on death or in life it might pass to a named third party.
3. Prior to the Perpetuities and Accumulations Act 1964 if resulting trust followed a determinable interest it was immune from perpetuity rule (though any express gift over was subject to it).
4. So a determinable charitable gift could terminate at a future point and result to settlor – no possibility of *cy-près* as no outright gift to charity.
5. S12 introduced a 'wait and see' rule – so in a determinable charitable gift a gift over or resulting trust operates and excludes *cy-près* providing it falls within perpetuity period – if not, gift is absolute and *cy-près* applies on subsequent failure.

8.12 STATUTORY *CY-PRÈS*

1. Before the Charities Act 1960, *cy-près* possible only if a gift failed for impossibility or impracticability of the purpose.
2. So *cy-près* could not be used to save a trust that had become uneconomic or outdated.
3. S13 passed to avoid this and was re-enacted in the 1993 Act.
4. S13(1) provides five circumstances where the purposes of a charitable gift can be altered to allow property to be reapplied under a *cy-près* scheme:
   (a) where the original purposes in whole or in part
      (i) have been as far as may be fulfilled; or
      (ii) cannot be carried out or not according to the dictates or spirit of the gift; or

(b) where the original purposes provide a use for part only of the property available by virtue of the gift; or

(c) where the property available by virtue of the gift and other property available for similar purposes can be more effectively used in conjunction and can suitably be made applicable to common purposes; or

(d) where the original purposes were laid down by reference to an area which then was but has since ceased to be suitable regard being had to the spirit of the gift or to practicality in administering the gift; or

(e) where the original purposes in whole or in part have since they were laid down
   (i) been adequately provided for by other means; or
   (ii) ceased as being useless or harmful to the community or for other reasons in law to be charitable; or
   (iii) ceased in any other way to provide a suitable and effective method of using the property available by virtue of the gift regard being had to the spirit of the gift.

5. So s13(2) provides that conditions other than impossibility have not been affected.

6. Width of charitable intent in case of subsequent failure is not significant – but Commissioners do try to adhere to settlor's intention, bearing in mind realities of current conditions.

7. First use of Act was to increase size of a gift where there was a surplus of funds (*Re Lepton's Charity* (1972)).

8. But s13 cannot be used for purely administrative changes (*Re J W Laing Trust* (1984)).

9. But may be used where current distribution of fund is inappropriate (*Peggs v Lamb* (1994)).

10. S14 overcomes difficulties where money is collected for a particular purpose that then proves to be unattainable and donors are then untraceable, e.g. flag days.

11. So *cy-près* shall be applied where the property belongs to:
    (a) a donor who after –
        (i) the prescribed advertisements and inquiries have been published and made, and
        (ii) the prescribed period beginning with the publication of the advertisements has expired – cannot be identified or cannot be found; or
    (b) a donor who has executed a disclaimer in the prescribed form for his right to have the property returned.

12. The Act also makes certain provisions for small charities:
    - charities with under £5,000 gross income and no land on trust may with agreement of two thirds of trustees transfer property to other charities if better use of resources – s74;
    - charities with a permanent endowment but no land and an income of under £1,000 may with agreement of two thirds of trustees remove restrictions on spending capital if income is too small to fulfil their purposes – s75.

Initial failure:
- Court must find wider charitable intent (*Re Rymer*).
- Usually gift fails for impossibility or impracticability (*Re Woodham*).
- Gift to specific charity saved if continued in new form (*Re Faraker*).
- Must distinguish between corporation and unincorporated association (*Re Vernon*).
- Easier if body never existed (*Re Harwood*).

Statutory *cy-près*:
- S13 CA 1993 – *cy-près* applies if gift
  (a) fulfilled or cannot be carried out;
  (b) purpose uses only part of fund;
  (c) gift can be more effectively used in other ways;
  (d) original purpose has ceased;
  (e) original purpose adequately provided for by other means, ceased to be charitable, or ceased to be suitable way of using gift.
- Cannot be used for purely administrative changes (*Re J W Laing Trust*)
- But possible for inappropriate distribution (*Peggs v Lamb*).
- S14 for donations, e.g. to disaster funds and donors cannot be found after proper advertising etc.
- Ss74 and 75 contain rules to redistribute really small funds.

CY-PRÈS

Subsequent failure:
- If gift fails after testator's death no need to find wider charitable intent (*Re Wright*).
- Because property trnsfers on death (*Re Slevin*).
- Surplus not so easy (*Re King*).

Who can be a trustee:
- Anyone who has capacity to hold property.
- Certain difficult ones which include – children (cannot own land); Crown (rarely); judicial trustees (where existing trust breaks down); Public Trustee (on intestacy); custodians (hold property only); trust corporations (e.g. solicitors)
- No maximum or minimum numbers – but should remember receipt rules.

Selection, appointment, vesting:
Court selection must acknowlege wishes of settlor; interests of all beneficiaries; efficient administration of trust; and avoid possible conflict of interests.

New trustees can be appointed by trust instrument; court under s36 TA 25 when proposed or existing trustees discharged, refuse, outside UK, incapable or unfit, die etc; be beneficiaries under TOLATA 96; by court under s41 TA 25 when trustee incapacitated by Mental Health Act 1983, or sole trustee dies, or is otherwise expedient.

Trustees cannot act till property is vested in them – can be automatic (s40 LPA 25).

NATURE OF TRUSTEESHIP

Standard of care:
Originally was standard or 'ordinary prudent businessman managing his own affairs' (*Speight v Gaunt*).

Professionals owed a higher standard of care (*Re Waterman's*).

Now by s1 TA 2000: 'must exercise such skill and care as it reasonable in all the circumstances' – And must have proper regard to special skills and whether acting professionally.

Duty applies to investment, acquiring property, appointing nominees and custodians, and insuring – but not maintenance and advancement.

Termination of trusteeship:
Disclaimer:
- Possible any time before act of acceptance.
- Usual by deed.

Death:
- Automatically terminates.
- Property vests in other trustees and personal representatives on death of last trustee.

Retirement:
- Discharges liability unless used to facilitate a breach.
- Can use express power in instrument, or court using s36 TA 25 (appointing replacement), or s39 (with no replacement), or s41 (where proper to allow retirement), or by beneficiaries under s19 TOLATA 96.

Removal:
- Court has inherent jurisdiction where trustee goes abroad, becomes unfit, goes bankrupt, or acts improperly.
- No need to show actual misconduct.

9.1 WHO CAN BE A TRUSTEE

1. In principle, anyone with capacity to own/hold property can be a trustee.
2. But certain classes of people require further consideration:
   - minors:
     - by Law of Property Act 1925 no minor can hold a legal estate in land – so cannot be a trustee of land;
     - but a minor may possibly act as trustee of personalty – or can be a resulting trustee (*Re Vinagradoff* (1935)).
   - The Crown:
     - can be a trustee in certain very rare circumstances;
     - but would need to state specifically that it acted as a trustee in private law – Lord Diplock in (*Town Investments Ltd v Department of the Environment* (1978)).
   - judicial trustees:
     - rare but possible under Judicial Trustee Rules 1983 – in absence of any fit and proper person
     - i.e. where administration by existing trustees breaks down.
   - the Public Trustee:
     - these have a variety of possible roles;
     - Including holding property of intestate deceased prior to the appointment of an administrator to the estate.
   - custodian trustees:
     - Public Trustee, Custodian for Charities, or a trust corporation;
     - can charge a fee – but not in excess of the proper fee charged by the Public Trustee;
     - hold property and documents – but leave day-to-day administration to the management trustees
   - trust corporations:
     - a common features of administrative trusts;

- banks, insurance companies, Public Trustee, Official Solicitor;
- capable of acting alone – where normal trustees could not, e.g. the overreaching mechanism;
- by TA 2000 now have general power to charge – before they would have relied on insertion of a charging clause in the trust instrument.

3. Nobody can be forced to act as trustee – though a resulting trustee is created by operation of law.
4. An intended trustee can always disclaim:
   - safest method is by deed;
   - but can be implied by acquiescence – to satisfaction of court;
   - any attempt to deal with estate classed as acceptance of role.

9.2 THE NUMBER OF TRUSTEES

1. There is no general maximum or minimum for personalty.
2. Usually taken to be no more than four in land (except in charities or pension funds) – because legal estate only vests in first four names.
3. By s14(2) TA 1925, impossible for sole trustee to give receipt for proceeds of sale arising from a trust of land or land under the Settled Land Act 1925.

9.3 APPOINTMENT OF TRUSTEES

1. First trustees can be appointed by settlor in trust instrument (though they do not have to accept office):
   - the gift will not fail merely because there are none;
   - the court will appoint trustees in that case.
2. Trustees hold as joint tenants – until retire or removed – when property vests in survivors: ss1–3 Administration of Estates Act 1925.

3. New trustees can be appointed through express powers in trust instrument – where such a power is expressly given to a specific person over and above the statutory powers.

4. New trustees can also be appointed by s36(1) and s36(2) TA 1925:
   - s36(1) lists circumstances where the power is required:
     - existing trustee is dead;
     - trustee remains outside of UK for 12 months or more;
     - trustee wishes to be discharged or refuses to take on role;
     - trustee is unfit to act or incapable of acting;
     - trustee is a minor.
   - then lists persons responsible for nominating trustees – if none available then surviving trustees or personal representatives can.

5. Beneficiaries can also appoint trustees under s19 TOLATA 96:
   - if all are of full age; and
   - all are absolutely entitled; and
   - all agree to the appointment.

6. The court can also appoint under s41 TA 1925:
   - when it is expedient to appoint only with help of court;
   - to replace trustee incapacitated by Mental Health Act 1983 order;
   - when sole trustee dies intestate or trustees predecease testator.

9.4 SELECTION OF TRUSTEES

1. Court appointing under s41 TA 1925 should take into account:
   - wishes of the settlor;
   - interests of all beneficiaries (and these may be conflicting);
   - the efficient administration of the trust.

2. Important for trustees to act together – but no veto for existing trustees.
3. Court should avoid appointment that would lead to conflict of interests, e.g. relative of a beneficiary, solicitor of trust (latter is not uncommon).
4. Offshore (foreign) trustees now rare – no longer same tax advantages.

9.5 THE VESTING OF THE TRUST PROPERTY

1. Trustees cannot act until the property is vested in them.
2. S40 Law of Property Act 1925 saves need for formal transfer – property automatically vested whenever appointment is made by deed.
3. Exceptions in s40(4): mortgage of land to secure loan of trust money; land held on lease with covenant against assignment without consent; stocks and shares.
4. Vesting orders also available to courts by ss44–56 LPA 1925.

9.6 TERMINATION OF TRUSTEESHIP

1. Can occur by – disclaimer, death, retirement, or removal.
2. Disclaimer:
   - any trustee can disclaim any time up to indicating acceptance;
   - but it is normal to disclaim by deed.
3. Death:
   - this automatically terminates trusteeship;
   - property vests in surviving trustees and personal representatives on last death.

4. Retirement:
   - discharges further responsibility and liability – unless retirement is used to facilitate a breach of trust in which case liability continues;
   - retirement can be achieved by various methods:
     - by an express power in the trust instrument;
     - by s36 TA 1925 when new trustee appointed for retiring one;
     - by s39 TA 1925, can retire even without a new appointment if:
       - does so in deed;
       - obtains consent of co-trustees by deed;
       - and two trustees or a trust corporation remains in place;
     - by an order of the court where it replaces a trustee under s41 TA 1925, or where it is proper to allow the trustee to retire;
     - by direction of the beneficiaries under s19 TOLATA 1996.

5. Removal:
   - the court has inherent jurisdiction to remove a trustee who:
     - takes up residence abroad;
     - refuses to act or is unfit to act or is incapable of acting;
     - becomes bankrupt;
     - behaves improperly although not in breach of trust.
   - no need to show actual misconduct – court must be satisfied continuing as trustee prejudices trust (*Moore v McGlynn* (1894)).

9.7 STANDARD OF CONDUCT EXPECTED OF TRUSTEES

1. Traditionally, the appropriate standard was that of the 'ordinary prudent businessman managing his own affairs' (*Speight v Gaunt* (1883)).

2. But now there is a statutory standard set in s1 Trustee Act 2000.

3. Even before 2000 Act, courts recognised that the standard must be higher for professional trustees (*Re Waterman's Will Trusts* (1952)).

4. Distinction maintained in s1 TA 2000: 'must exercise such skill and care as is reasonable in all the circumstances, having regard in particular (a) to any special knowledge or experience that he has or holds himself out as having, and (b) if he acts as trustee in the course of a business or profession, to any special knowledge or experience that it is reasonable to expect of a person acting in the course of that kind of business or profession'.

5. The standard applies to various functions exercised by the trustee:
   - investment;
   - acquiring land;
   - appointing nominees and custodians;
   - insuring property.

6. But not to, e.g. exercise powers of maintenance and advancement.

7. So duty concerns way power exercised not whether discretion used.

8. On the contrary, a failure to exercise a duty leads to a breach of trust.

9. Trustees not liable by s61 TA 1925 if acted 'honestly and reasonably'.

10. TA 2000 does not specifically deal with trustee exemption clauses but the statutory will only not apply 'if or insofar as it appears from the trust instrument that the duty is not meant to apply'.

11. Even express exemption will not protect a trustee in cases of bad faith, recklessness, or deliberate breach of a duty – because to allow exemption in such cases would offend public policy.

12. But a trustee might be protected against a claim of gross negligence under an express clause (*Armitage v Nurse* (1998)).

13. However, must still comply with s2(3) Unfair Contract Terms Act 1977.

14. Trustees can make contracts with third parties – but these are generally not enforceable by the third parties against the trust assets.

CHAPTER 10
THE DUTIES OF THE TRUSTEES

General duties to the trust property:
To collect assets:
- New trustee must check state of investments and ensure all property is vested in trustees.
- To safefuard trust (*Re Brogden*).

To distribute fund correctly:
- Must pay income or capital as it becomes due to beneficiaries.
- Or make payment into court if beneficiaries cannot be found (*Re Gillingham Bus Disaster Fund*).
- Or distribute after seeking Benjamin Orders.

The duty to invest
- Investment is 'anything from which interest or profit is expected' (*Re Wragg*).
- Complex history of rules through 1925 Act and 1961 Trustee Investment Act because of specualtive nature of equities and land.
- Now rules are in Part II TA 2000 – can make any investment as if absolute owner of fund.
- General power in s3 additional to any express power in trust instrument.
- Power to provide mortgages of land or invest in land in ss3 and 8
- Must follow 'standard investment criteria in s4 – and be aware of need for diversification – 'portfolio theory'.
- Should take advice by s5 – need not be written.
- Can delegate investment powers – and use custodians s16, and nominees s17.
- Original standard of care – that in *Learoyd v Whiteley* – reasonable prudent businessman test – now in s1 – what is reasonable in all circumstances – and standard is more stringent if a professional trustee.

TRUSTEE DUTIES

General duties to the beneficiaries:
Duty to convert:
- Must maintain equality between beneficiaries (*Lloyds Bank v Duker*).
- So must take equal view of income for life tenant and capital for remainderman.
- And sell unauthorised or wasting assets to 'convert' to authorised – rule in *How v Dartmouth* unless stated contrary in will.

Duty to apportion:
- Builds on conversion to apportion funds appropriately between income and capital.

Duty to provide accounts.

Fiduciary nature of trusteeship:
- Basic principle in *Bray v Ford* – trustee must not allow interest and duty to conflict.
- So remuneration only possible if authorised, e.g. in trust instrument (charging clauses) or by court, statutory authorisation or by beneficiaries.
- Must not buy trust property – except if independent of trust (*Holder v Holder*).
- Must not make a secret or incidental profit (*Boardman v Phipps*).
- Rule strict – so applies even though does not harm trust and even benefits it.
- Only significant point is that fiduciary gained personal benefit from his position as fiduciary.
- Can be liable to account for renewing lease owned by trust in own name (*Keech v Sandford*).
- Or for taking freehold reversion in own name (*Protheroe v Protheroe*).
- Applies equally to directors coming by benefits (*Regal (Hastings) v Gulliver*).
- Even when knowledge came in personal capacity but is usful to company (*IDC v Cooley*).
- But Upjohn in *Boardman* felt it unfairly decided.

10.1 THE TRUSTEES' DUTIES TO THE TRUST PROPERTY

10.1.1 The duty to collect assets

1. On first appointment a trustee must:
   - familiarise himself with the terms of the trust;
   - check the state of the investments;
   - ensure that all property is vested in his and other trustees' names;
   - if a replacement trustee, check nothing amounting to breach of trust remains from the previous trustee.
2. One purpose of checks is to ensure trust is safeguarded – a continuing and stringent obligation (*Re Brogden* (1888)).
3. Duty is so strict that a trustee might be bound to break his word in order to protect trust (*Buttle v Saunders* (1950)).
4. So trustees may have to use litigation to protect trust.
5. But can take costs from fund unless: litigation arose from trustee's breach; litigation was speculative and unsuccessful; or trustee acted in a hostile way towards beneficiaries.

10.1.2 The duty to distribute

1. Trustee must pay income and capital as they become due – failure to do so is breach and trustee is personally liable.
2. If trustee overpays a beneficiary, this can be adjusted in later payments.
3. If trustee pays a person not entitled, remedy is in quasi-contract – so beneficiary can proceed against that person as well as trustee – subject to the doctrine of notice (*Re Diplock*).
4. If trustee is in doubt re a beneficiary's claim, then he can seek directions from court.
5. If beneficiaries cannot be found then trustees can make payment into court to discharge themselves (*Gillingham Bus Disaster Fund* (1959)).

6. Courts may also make 'Benjamin orders' – so that fund can be distributed and later claims would be against those over-endowed, not the trustees (*Re Green's Will Trusts* (1985)).

7. Trustees may advertise for claimants by s27 TA 1925 following certain formalities.

8. Trustee may be protected by s61 TA 1925 if he acted honestly and reasonably.

9. Best way for trustees to discharge themselves is to obtain a release deed from beneficiaries after providing final account.

10.2 THE DUTY TO INVEST

10.2.1 The basis of the duty

1. Duty to invest is part of trustee's duty to safeguard and protect trust.

2. Investment is not defined in Trustee Act 2000 – nor in Law Commission Report No 260 (1999) *Trustees' Powers and Duties* that preceded it – but Lawrence J in *Re Wragg* defined it as 'to employ money in the purchase of anything from which interest or profit is expected'.

3. Report No 260 identified investment as 'an evolving concept' that could be 'capital appreciation rather than income yield'.

4. Investment inevitably affects life tenants (interest is in income) and remaindermen (interest is in capital) – so trustee must be careful not to advantage one at expense of other.

5. Trustees must operate within powers of investment granted either in the trust instrument or by the courts, or from statute.

6. Trustees are also bound by the duty of care, originally at common law, but now in s1 TA 2000.

10.2.2 The types of investment

1. Basically two different types which incorporate all others:
   - a loan at a rate of interest;
   - a profit making activity, an equity.
2. In general, though, there is a confusing array of potential investments – some relatively safe with low interest rates, some more speculative with higher interest.
3. Loans at a rate – can include:
   - bank and building society deposit accounts – with variable interest rates;
   - government/local authority stock – usually fixed interest;
   - debentures – loans to companies, supported by a floating charge on assets of company (leaving company free to deal with assets) – value depends on current commercial viability of company;
   - preference shares – have preference over ordinary shares in relation to payment of dividends.
4. Equities can include:
   - ordinary shares in a company – return may be good if company performs well, but disastrous if it performs badly – the reason why they were prohibited under the Trustee Investments Act 1971;
   - unit trusts – investment spread over range of companies, managed by investment experts as a single fund divided into units;
   - investment trusts – a company in which shares are bought which then invests in shares in other companies itself – return being dividend from investment trust.
5. Pension funds sometimes take advantage of 'derivatives' (made up of 'futures' and 'options' – so potentially very high yield but very risky) – but most trusts could not invest in them.
6. Trustees' only real consideration when deciding on a particular investment is that the financial benefits should be maximized – they must not be influenced by others.

10.2.3 Express investment powers

1. In the past, wide investment powers were commonly drafted into trust instrument by testator.
2. This would be essentially for two reasons:
   - investment powers prior to and included in the 1961 Act were felt to be very narrow and restrictive;
   - procedures required by the 1961 Act were felt to be overcomplicated and expensive to comply with.
3. Wider powers of investment in Part II TA 2000 (to make any investment as if absolutely entitled to fund) may make express clauses unnecessary, except to restrict or exclude statutory power
4. At one time, express clauses were construed very strictly – so as only to allow trustees to invest in those securities authorised by general law
5. But relaxed in *Re Harrari's Settlement Trusts* (1949) – where words 'in or upon such investments as to them may seem fit' were held to include equities.

10.2.4 Development of statutory powers of investment

1. Originally rules on investment were aimed at avoiding all risk to capital of fund – and founded on idea that there would be little inflation – only investment in fixed government securities was originally permitted.
2. The 1925 Act liberalised this to an extent – but still only allowed investment in 'narrow range' – with no power to invest in equities or in land.
3. Trustee Investment Act 1961 passed to modernise law and allow limited scope to invest in equities and land – and to give more flexibility to trustees:
   - trustees could originally invest half of fund in equities;
   - later increased to three quarters by Trustee Investments (Division of Trust Fund) Order 1996;

- but Act was complicated to apply – fund literally had to be divided before trustees were safe to invest – and complex rules regarding when withdrawing funds from trust – and out of date with general investment practice.
4. Law Commission recognised the limitations and need for reform – as did Treasury consultation paper: *Investment Powers of Trustees 1996* – so expanding investment powers was a major purpose of the 2000 Act.

10.2.5 Powers of Investment under Trustee Act 2000

1. Basic investment power is in s3(1): 'a trustee may make any kind of investment that he could make if he were absolutely entitled to the assets of the trust':
   - described in s3(2) as the 'general power of investment' – appropriate to any trust;
   - general power is in addition to any express power;
   - but does not apply to trusts of pension funds, unit trusts, or charities;
   - by s3(4) limited power to provide mortgages of land under 1925 and 1961 Acts is replaced by general power to invest in land by way of loans secured against the land by legal mortgage.
2. Trustees could not formerly invest in land without express power:
   - and purchasing a house for a beneficiary to live in not originally possible as an investment (*Re Power* (1947));
   - s6(3) Trusts of Land and Appointment of Trustees Act 1996 gave trustees powers to purchase legal estate in land – under s6(4) this was for: investment; occupation by a beneficiary; or any other purpose;
   - now widened by s8 TA 2000 – subject to any exclusion or restriction in trust, trustees may acquire freehold or leasehold land in UK for same purposes as above – and trustee for this purpose has all powers of absolute owner.

3. S4 sets out the 'standard investment criteria':
   - must be followed when exercising investment powers:
     (a) the suitability to the trust of investments of same kind as any particular investments proposed to be made or retained and of that particular investment of that kind; and
     (b) the need for diversification of investments of the trust, insofar as is appropriate to the circumstances of the trust
   - trustees should review investments from time to time – and in light of standard investment criteria, consider whether or not are appropriate or should be varied;
   - trustees should also take into account 'portfolio theory' – investments should not be seen in isolation but as part of an overall strategy of investment.

4. Advice may still be needed as it formerly was:
   - by s5, trustee should when reviewing investments or exercising investment powers obtain and consider 'proper advice';
   - 'proper advice' is that believed by trustees to be from those qualified to give it, having regard to investments;
   - unlike 1961 Act, no need for advice to be in writing;
   - by s3, trustee need not seek advice where in all the circumstances he believes it unnecessary/inappropriate.

5. Delegation of trustee powers not originally possible (except with express permission – as involved delegating discretion):
   - trustees had to apply to court for extension of powers or could delegate by power of attorney under s25 TA 1925;
   - now TA 2000 permits delegation by listing in s11 all those functions that may not be delegated;
   - s16 allows for nominees to be appointed;
   - s17 allows for custodians to be appointed;
   - whenever trustees delegate to nominees, custodians or agents they must keep the arrangement under review;
   - statutory duty applies to appointment and functions.

6. Duty of care owed by trustees formerly set by common law:
   - In *Learoyd v Whiteley* (1886) Lord Lindley MR said:
     'The duty is not to take such care only as a prudent
     man of business would take if he only had himself to
     consider; the duty rather is take such care as an ordinary
     prudent man of business would take if he were minded
     to make an investment for the benefit of other people
     for whom he felt morally bound to provide.'
   - and the duty is also to act fairly between all beneficiaries
     (*Bartlett v Barclays Bank plc* (1980));
   - and also to do the best financially that can be done for
     the beneficiaries (*Cowan v Scargill* (1984));
   - now under s1 2000 Act trustee 'must exercise such care
     and skill as is reasonable in the circumstances, having
     regard in particular (a) to any special knowledge or
     experience that he has or holds himself out as having,
     and (b) if he acts as a trustee in the course of a business
     or profession, to any special knowledge or experience
     that it is reasonable to expect of a person acting in the
     course of that kind of business or profession'.

10.2.6 Choice of investment

1. Following 2000 Act, the trustee must still avoid
   investments 'which are attended with hazard'.
2. Trustee who commits an error of judgment is not likely to
   be held in breach of trust (*Nestlé v National Westminster
   Bank plc* (1993)).
3. So trustees may pursue an 'ethical' investment policy as
   long as it is also as financially sound as any alternatives
   (*Martin v City of Edinburgh District Council* (1998)).
4. And in charitable trusts trustees may in any case need to be
   satisfied that investment is in line with objectives of charity
   (*Harries v Church Commissioners for England* (1992)).
5. The trust instrument may also provide for 'ethical'
   investment.

10.3 THE TRUSTEES' DUTIES TO THE BENEFICIARIES

10.3.1 The duty to convert

1. The first duty of the trustee to the beneficiaries is to maintain equality between them (*Lloyds Bank plc v Duker* (1987)).
2. The duty to convert arises where beneficiaries are entitled in succession:
   - life tenant has immediate use of property plus income;
   - the remainderman is entitled to the capital only after the life tenant's death;
   - so injustice would result unless investment is balanced – too speculative and fund might be dissipated at expense of remainderman, too cautious and fund might be preserved at expense of life tenant's income.
3. The duty to convert is to sell certain unauthorised assets to buy authorised ones.
4. Called rule in *Howe v Dartmouth* (1802) – that, unless there is a contrary provision made in the will, where residual personalty is settled in succession, trustees must 'convert':
   - any asset of a wasting nature;
   - any asset of a reversionary nature;
   - any unauthorised investments.
5. Rule has limited application as does not apply to:
   - lifetime settlements;
   - specific or general bequests rather than a residuary gift;
   - leasehold land;
   - where the rule is expressly or impliedly excluded, e.g. a provision that nothing in the estate should be sold.

10.3.2 The duty to apportion

1. This duty arises also when there is a duty to convert.

2. Reason is to ensure income derived from unauthorised investments is then fairly distributed between capital and income – so both life tenant and remainderman fairly treated.

3. In case of wasting, hazardous, or unauthorised investments assumption is that these unfairly favour the life tenant:
   - so apportionment ensures life tenant receives an income representing the current yield on authorised investments;
   - currently 4% – but out of line with accurate yield;
   - if there is no power to postpone then trustees should convert within one year (the time expected for full administration) – assets sold within a year are valued at time of sale, otherwise value after one year is taken;
   - if there is a power to postpone then value is taken as from the testator's death (*Brown v Gellatly* (1867)).

4. For future, reversionary, or other non-income producing property apportionment necessary to protect life tenant who otherwise gains no benefit.

5. Possible to avoid rules if contrary intention shown by testator.

6. Also solicitors on making wills usually exclude the rule in *Howe v Dartmouth*.

7. Law Reform Committee 23rd Report 1982 suggested a statutory rule rather than replacing rule altogether – would place duty on trustee to hold fair balance between life tenant and remainderman.

8. Other rules also deal with apportionment:
   - the Apportionment Act 1870 concerns dividing income, profit, rents etc unpaid at time of testator's death;
   - the rule in *Allhusen v Whittell* (1867) – because the life tenant should only take an income net of testator's debts, then he is obliged to make a contribution.

10.3.3 The duty to provide accounts and information

1. Trustees owe duty to keep accurate and up-to-date accounts.
2. Beneficiary entitled to inspect accounts but no right to a copy.
3. Remainderman only entitled to capital accounts relating to his reversion – life tenant entitled to full accounts.
4. Discretionary beneficiary may see accounts – but not a potential discretionary beneficiary.
5. Charitable trusts and pension funds require proper audited accounts.
6. Other trusts usually do not – but trustees may have them audited and charge fund – but only occasionally not annually.
7. Beneficiaries are also entitled to be informed of matters currently affecting the trust (for charities there is a statutory list) – with private trusts this might generally include:
   - documents in possession of trustees acting as trustees;
   - documents containing information on the trust that beneficiaries are entitled to know about.
8. *Re Londonderry's Settlement* (1965) – the beneficiaries have a proprietary interest in these documents.
9. Beneficiary may be denied access to testator's confidential wishes (*Hartigan Nominees Pty Ltd v Ridge* (1992)).

10.4 THE FIDUCIARY NATURE OF TRUSTEESHIP

10.4.1 Remuneration and reimbursement of trustees

1. Basic principle trustee is volunteer – so no payment.
2. So can only receive remuneration if specifically entitled.

3. But trustee can use lien over trust fund to recover out-of-pocket expenses, e.g. agent's fees, proper costs of litigation.
4. The right to reimbursement is statutory – s31 TA 2000.
5. Numerous ways that remuneration may be authorised:
   - in the trust instrument itself:
     - commonly in 'charging clauses' before the 2000 Act;
     - now by s28 an express clause will be upheld even if it is possible to use a lay (and thus free) trustee;
   - under TA 2000:
     - Part V gives professional trustees right to take remuneration even if not expressly provided for;
     - by s29 they may take 'a reasonable remuneration';
     - but sole trustees excluded as no scrutiny possible;
   - other statutory authorisation:
     - Public Trustees entitled under s9 Public Trustees Act 1906;
     - judicial trustees are entitled under s1 Judicial Trustees Act 1898;
     - corporations appointed as Custodian Trustees are entitled by s4 Public Trustees Act 1906;
   - authorisation by the court:
     - court has inherent jurisdiction exercisable retrospectively or prospectively when work of trustee (fiduciary) (even one in breach of trust) has been of significant value to trust (*Boardman v Phipps* (1967));
     - can also use this jurisdiction if trustee has used specialist skills and would not have if aware there would be no remuneration (*Foster v Spencer* (1996));
     - courts do not usually use inherent jurisdiction in respect of directors because of likelihood of conflict of interest and duty (*Guiness v Saunders* (1990));
   - remuneration for litigious work by solicitor trustees:
     - the so-called rule in (*Craddock v Piper* (1850));
     - whereby a solicitor may charge costs where he has acted for a co-trustee as well as himself;

- Contracts with *sui juris* beneficiaries for payment. possible.

10.4.2 Trustees as purchasers of trust property

1. Trustees should not become owners or lessees of trust property – this is to avoid any potential conflict of interest – and it is irrelevant that a fair price is paid.
2. Though the rule has been somewhat relaxed – where there is clearly no conflict of interest (*Holder v Holder* (1968)).
3. Should not even buy property a long time after retiring.
4. But possible for trustee to buy beneficial interest providing that there is no undue influence (*Tito v Waddell (No 2)* (1977)).

10.4.3 Trustees and incidental (secret) profits

1. According to Lord Herschell in *Bray v Ford* (1896), 'it is an inflexible rule of equity that a person in a fiduciary position ... is not, unless otherwise expressly provided, entitled to make a profit; he is not allowed to put himself in a position where his interest and his duty conflict'.
2. So this is the logic behind the twin rule that trustee must not:
   - be paid for his services without express authorisation;
   - make any kind of secret profit from the trust.
3. Rule in *Keech v Sanford* (1726) prevents trustee renewing in his own name a lease he held formerly as a trustee.
4. But applies only to fiduciaries (*Re Biss* (1903)).
5. If trustee acquires freehold reversion then may be liable if used his position as trustee to gain personal benefit (*Protheroe v Protheroe* (1968)).
6. Where directors have received their positions by result of their being trustees then they may be liable to the trust for money they receive (*Re Macadam* (1946)).

7. But they may keep remuneration if they were directors before being trustees (*Re Dover Coalfield Extension Ltd* (1908)).

8. Basic rule is – however trustee comes by profit, if made as result of position as trustee then must account to trust for it

9. Trustee must never compete with trust (*Re Thompson* (1930)).

10. *Bray v Ford* applies to fiduciaries generally, not just trustees.

11. One major problem is identifying fiduciary relationship – some obvious ones such as solicitor and client, agents and their principals, directors and shareholders, partners:
   - but list not fixed and courts do label someone a fiduciary merely for desired result (*Reading v A-G* (1951));
   - or deny relationship (*Swain v The Law Society* (1983)).

12. Company directors are identified as fiduciaries – so are prevented from using knowledge gained in office for private gain *Regal (Hastings) Ltd v Gulliver (1967)*

13. This point has been extended so that directors have even been held liable for profit made using knowledge gained in a personal capacity if it could have been used by the company *Industrial Development Consultants Ltd v Cooley (1972)*

14. Leading case, demonstrating how rigidly principle applies, is *Boardman v Phipps* (1967):
   - the case involved one beneficiary and the trust solicitor;
   - latter held to account as fiduciary, not as trustee – though Lords were split on whether he acted in a private capacity;
   - fact trust lost nothing and actually gained held irrelevant;
   - Lord Upjohn (dissenting) felt principle of preventing conflict of interest and duty wrongly applied – called it 'unreasonable and inequitable application of such doctrines';

- other problem was who fiduciary owes duty to, trust or beneficiaries (consent obtained from two active trustees) – position now modified by TA 2000 which authorises conflicts of interests if necessary for benefit of trust.

15. In comparison to *Boardman*, Commonwealth courts are less hostile to fiduciaries (*Queensland Mines Ltd v Hudson* (1978)) – similar to dissenting judgments of Lords Upjohn and Dilhorne in *Boardman*.

CHAPTER 11

THE POWERS OF TRUSTEES

Trusts of land:
- By s6 TOLATA trustee of land has all rights of absolute owner.
- Applies to express or implied trusts
- Further powers include – to transfer property, or to partition – in either case with consent of adult beneficiaries all in agreement.

General powers:
All powers are discretionary – general powers include:
- To sell trust property – s6 TOLATA for land – or s12 TA 25 – but must obtain best price (*Buttle v Saunders*).
- To give receipts – s14 TA 25, e.g. for overreaching.
- To insure – s19 TA 2000 – money recovered must be treated as capital and applied accordingly.
- To compound liabilities.

POWERS OF TRUSTEES

Maintenance and advancement:
Discretionary powers not subject to TA duty of care.
Maintenance = s31 TA 25 beneficiary with vested or contingent interest – either before 18 or after if contingency not yet met – trustee can apply income for, e.g. support, education, etc.
- Only possible if not prior claim, e.g. life interest.
- Can be expressly denied in trust instrument (*Re Turner's Will Trusts*).
- Only applies to gifts carrying with them the intermediate income – vested gifts; contingent residuary personalty; but not contingent pecuniary unless – settlor is father of child, intention shown in instrument (*Re Churchill*) or separate sum set aside (*Re Medlock*).
Advancement = s32 TA 25 beneficiary with unmet continent interest – trustee can apply capital; to 'set beneficiary up in life' – examples in *Pilkington v IRC*:
- Only half of presumptive share can be applied.
- Share advanced is set off against entitlement.
- Must not disadvantage person with prior interest unless adult and consents in writing.
- Contrary intention can be shown in instrument.
- Provision for accumulation precludes advancement.
- Must ensure that advance is supervised (*Re Pauling's Settlement Trusts*).

Power to delegate:
- Originally possible only if necessary and conforms with standard business practice (*Speight v Gaunt*).
- Must be careful in selection (*Fry v Tapson*).
- S23 TA 25 gave indemnity to trustee who delegated in good faith.
- S30 protected trustee against loss caused other than by his wilful default.
- Scope of protection uncertain – compare *Re Vickery* and *Re Luckings*.
- Now TA 2000 gives wider power to delegate.
- Can delegate functions other than those in s11: distribution of fund, maintenance and advancement, appointment of new trustees.
- By s16 trustees can appoint nominees and by s17 custodians.
- Some delegation of discretion possible, e.g. s9 TOLATA.

11.1 INTRODUCTION

1. Powers must be distinguished from duties – because there are significant consequences depending on whether something is one rather than the other:
   - duties are obligatory – and failure to comply can lead to breach of trust actions;
   - powers are discretionary – so there is no compulsion other than to exercise the discretion.
2. Powers of trustee were originally identified in trust instrument:
   - but TA 1925 gave detail on powers needed by all trustees;
   - but Act became outdated re powers of delegation, insurance, remuneration, investment, appointing nominees and custodians;
   - so most of these areas are now updated in Trustee Act 2000.
3. Certain significant powers are enjoyed by trustees:
   - to sell the property to use the fund in different ways;
   - to give receipts to purchasers to enable overreaching mechanism;
   - powers in respect of liability to the trust or by the trust;
   - powers in relation to reversionary interests.
4. But the two major powers are:
   - delegation;
   - maintenance and advancement.

11.2 TRUSTEES OF LAND UNDER THE TRUSTS OF LAND AND APPOINTMENT OF TRUSTEES ACT 1996

1. By s6(1) TOLATA trustees of land are given 'all of the powers of an absolute owner' (formerly trustees of a trust for sale had a duty to sell with only a power to postpone).

2. So trustee now has greater flexibility – but must still:
   - give proper regard to rights of beneficiaries and there is a duty to consult adult beneficiaries in possession of the land;
   - maintain all general duties and all statutory restrictions.
3. S6 applies to any trust of land whether express or implied – though an express trust of land may be excluded by the settlor.
4. Two further major powers within the Act:
   - trustees have power to transfer trust property where adult beneficiaries of full capacity acting together call for a transfer;
   - trustees can partition lands when consented to by beneficiaries and they are all adult and absolutely entitled as tenants in common.

11.3 GENERAL POWERS

11.3.1 The power to sell trust property

1. By s6(1) TOLATA trustees of a trust of land (or post-1996 settlement) are vested with the legal estate and thus have power to sell.
2. For pre-1996 settlements the legal estate is vested in the tenant for life who thus has the power of sale.
3. For overreaching to occur the receipt of two trustees or a trust corporation must be obtained by purchasers.
4. Power of sale exists for chattels and receipt of only a single trustee is needed.
5. Power of sale often implied in case of unauthorised investments which are not suitable for trust – and should be sold and replaced in more permanent form:
   - Trustee Act 2000 puts this into statutory form;
   - trustees may also mortgage property to raise money for authorised purposes.

6. Rules on sale of trust property are in s12 TA 1925:
   - can sell all or any of trust property by public auction or private sale;
   - can subject any sale to conditions;
   - but have duty to obtain best possible price (*Buttle v Saunders*) – beneficiary can restrain by injunction a sale that does not do this.

11.3.2 The power to give receipts

1. By s14 TA 1926 trustees may give receipts for money, securities, investments etc sold.
2. Receipt protects purchaser from liability to beneficiaries for misapplication of fund.
3. Applies irrespective of any contrary statement in trust instrument and can apply to sole trustees.
4. S14 applies other than to proceeds of sale of a trust of land or settled land under SLA 1925 when receipt of two trustees or trust corporation is needed to evoke overreaching mechanism to protect purchaser.

11.3.3 The power to insure

1. At common law there is a power to insure – which in any case is one way of safeguarding the trust property.
2. By s19 TA 1925 trustees were also given limited powers to insure – now under s19 Trustee Act 2000:
   - the trustee may insure against any risks;
   - and may pay the premiums from capital.
3. The statutory duty of care from s1 TA 2000 applies.
4. Money recovered from policies must be treated as capital and applied accordingly.

11.3.4 The power to compound liabilities

1. By s15 TA 1925 settlement can be made with any person claiming to be a beneficiary.

2. And trustee can adjust interests between competing beneficiaries – to reach a sensible compromise instead of facing litigation in every competing claim.

3. Providing they comply with the statutory duty of care, trustees will not be liable for loss caused by exercising their powers under s15.

11.4 THE POWER TO DELEGATE

1. The original common law rule is that a trustee will not be liable for the faults of another to whom he has delegated functions.

2. In practice, trustees need to delegate all manner of functions – recognised as early as *ex parte Belchier* (1754).

3. Trustees traditionally could delegate only where necessary and when delegation conforms with standard business practice (*Speight v Gaunt* (1883)) and where they act as reasonable prudent businessmen (*Learoyd v Whiteley* (1887)).

4. Trustees must also employ the 'agent' in the course of their business and must take care in selecting them – and originally could not delegate discretionary powers (*Fry v Tapson* (1884)).

5. So in 19th century commonplace to insert express delegation powers with exemption for trustees from anything except their wilful default

6. Wide powers of delegation powers were granted in 23(1) TA 1925: 'trustees ... may instead of acting personally employ ... an agent whether a solicitor, banker, stockbroker or other person to ... do any act ... in the execution of the trust or the administration of an estate ... and shall not be liable for the default of any such agent if employed in good faith.'

7. Similarly, s30 TA 1925 created an indemnity for acts and defaults of agents unless loss caused through trustees' 'wilful default'.

8. Exact scope of provisions was uncertain and case law contradictory – compare *Re Vickery* (1931) where there was said to be no liability unless trustee acted with wilful default, with *Re Lucking's Will Trusts* (1968) where court said trustee was allowed to delegate but had a corresponding duty to supervise.

9. Where s23 did not permit delegation of discretions this was permissible by power of attorney under s25.

10. Trustee Act 2000 passed to repeal these and provide clear framework.

11. The Act widens powers of delegation but can still be subject to restrictions in the trust instrument.

12. In effect trustees can delegate all or any delegable functions other than those in s11:
    ● those relating to how assets should be distributed;
    ● decisions on whether payments should be from income or capital;
    ● power to appoint new trustees;
    ● any power conferred by other enactment permitting trustees to delegate functions or to appoint custodians or nominees.

13. So significantly allows for delegation of investment powers to experts.

14. Functions delegable in charitable trusts are also listed.

15. By s16 trustees can appoint nominees and by s17 custodians – so prevents delays in transferring shares.

16. Trustee must maintain statutory duty of care under s1 when delegating – which applies to supervision as well as appointing.

17. Under s23 TA 2000 trustee is not liable for acts of agent, nominee or custodian unless he has failed to comply with the duty of care both in appointing and supervision.

18. Some delegation of discretion is permitted:
    ● by s9 TOLATA 1996 trustee of trust of land can delegate any functions relating to land, including sale to beneficiaries of full age;

- under s1 Trustee Delegation Act 1999 trustee of trust of land can delegate all functions, including discretions, by power of attorney;
- s25 TA 1925 in any case allowed for delegation of powers and discretions either by deed or by power of attorney.

11.5 POWERS OF MAINTENANCE AND ADVANCEMENT

11.5.1 Introduction

1. Maintenance and advancement covers situations where a beneficiary will not receive until a set date in the future but wants support now.
2. Maintenance is when trustees allow a beneficiary money from income.
3. Advancement is when trustees allow a contingent beneficiary money from capital.
4. There are a variety of reasons for doing so:
   - commonly for tax saving;
   - for contingent interests no use is made of the intermediate income so it is a way of using it for the immediate benefit of the beneficiary;
   - it can also help children with vested interests.
5. Neither power significantly is subject to the statutory duty of care.
6. Both should result from conscious exercise of trustees' discretion – not automatic right – and it does not matter that other parties are benefited.

11.5.2 Maintenance

1. The power derives from the trust instrument or from s31 TA 1925:
   'Where any property is held by trustees in trust for any person for any interest whatsoever, whether vested or

contingent, then, subject to any prior interests or charges affecting that property –

(i) during the infancy of any such person, if his interest so long continues, the trustees may, at their sole discretion, pay to his parent or guardian, if any, or otherwise apply for or towards his maintenance or education or benefit, the whole or such part, if any, of the income of that property as may, in all the circumstances, be reasonable whether or not there is –
a) any other fund applicable for the same purposes; or
b) any person bound by law to provide for his maintenance or education; and

(ii) if such person attaining the age of [18] years has not a vested interest in such income, the trustees shall thenceforth pay the income of that property and of any accretion thereto under subsection (2) of this section to him until he either attains a vested interest or dies, or until failure of his interest …'

2. So trustees can use their discretion to support a minor beneficiary with either a vested or contingent interest.

3. And even after the minor reaches 18 the income can still be used to support him if he has a contingent interest.

4. Decision to grant should result from conscious exercise of discretion – so not a right – and will not matter that someone else benefits.

5. Once beneficiary meets the contingency he is also entitled to the capital.

6. By s53 TA 1925 application can be made to the court where the trust instrument does not provide for maintenance.

7. Maintenance only possible where no prior interest, e.g. a life interest.

8. A contrary intent can always be expressed in the trust instrument – and may be construed, e.g. from a direction to accumulate (*Re Turner's Will Trusts* (1937)).

9. By s31(2) surplus income is accumulated for child beneficiaries till they reach majority:
   - child is entitled to accumulations if he has a vested interest before reaching majority – because then he is in any case entitled to the income;
   - but principle may not apply if there is an express contrary intention in trust instrument (*Re Delamere's Settlement Trusts* (1984)).

10. S31 only applies to gifts that carry with them entitlement to the intermediate income – though it is not absolutely clear which gifts do and which do not:
    - vested gifts always carry the intermediate income unless contrary intent is shown;
    - with contingent residuary gifts of personalty, intermediate income is said to attach to beneficiary unless a contrary intention is shown;
    - with a contingent pecuniary legacy this will not usually carry with it intermediate income on basis that a bequest of a fixed amount means testator only intended that amount to pass to beneficiary – but there are three exceptions:
      (i) where the settlor is the father of the child;
      (ii) where intention to maintain is shown (*Re Churchill* (1909));
      (iii) where testator has set aside the legacy as distinct and separate fund for beneficiary (*Re Medlock* (1886)).

11. In a contingent gift for a class of beneficiaries maintenance can still be given to those beneficiaries who do not yet have a vested interest even though some of the class have met their contingency.

12. If a member of a class dies before his interest is vested, accumulation of interests representing his contingent interest is added to the capital.

11.5.3 Advancement

1. Where maintenance concerns application of income to support a child beneficiary's needs advancement is application of capital before the minor is actually entitled.

2. Advancement is authorised in the trust instrument or in s32 TA 1925:

   'Trustees may at any time or times pay or apply any capital money subject to a trust, for the advancement or benefit, in such manner as they may, in their absolute discretion, think fit, of any person entitled to the capital of the trust property or of any share thereof, whether absolutely or contingently on his attaining any specified age or on the occurrence of any other event, and whether in possession or in remainder or reversion, and such payment or application may be made notwithstanding that the interest of such person is liable to be defeated by the exercise of a power of appointment or revocation, or to be diminished by the increase of the class to which he belongs:

   Provided that –

   (a) the money so paid or applied for the advancement or benefit of any person shall not exceed altogether in amount one half of the presumptive or vested share or interest of that person in the trust property; and

   (b) if that person is or becomes absolutely and indefeasibly entitled to a share in the trust property the money so paid or applied shall be brought into account as part of such share; and

   (c) no such payment or application shall be made so as to prejudice any person entitled to any prior life or other interest, whether vested or contingent, in the money paid or applied unless such person is in existence and of full, age and consents in writing to such payment or application.'

3. As with maintenance a major purpose of applying the money is tax saving but generally the purpose is 'the

establishment in life of the beneficiary ... or some step that
will contribute to the furtherance of his establishment':
Jessel MR in *Taylor v Taylor* (1875).

4. Traditional examples of advancement were:
   - buying an apprenticeship for a young person;
   - buying a commission in the armed forces;
   - buying young person share in business, company or
     partnership;
   - helping a person to get started at the Bar;
   - enabling a woman to marry.

5. More modern examples include:
   - paying off debts;
   - providing for a charity;
   - providing the means of supporting a wife or children or
     both.

6. Many of these were discussed in *Pilkington v IRC* (1964) in
   which it was also identified that any other way of
   improving the material situation of the beneficiary is
   acceptable.

7. The scope of express powers of advancement was
   traditionally construed quite narrowly – so it was practice
   in drafting such clauses to include words to widen the
   scope, e.g. 'for the advancement of or otherwise for his
   benefit'.

8. In practice since TA 1925 any express provision would only
   add to the whole of the beneficiary's presumptive share.

9. S32 TA 1925 is the major process for advancement – with
   many important features:
   - it obviously means money can be applied from capital
     regardless of whether beneficiary's interest is vested or
     contingent;
   - decision to apply capital for advancement is at trustees'
     discretion;
   - only half of the presumptive share can be applied;
   - share advanced is set off against entitlement when
     received;

- advancement must not disadvantage a person with a prior interest unless that person is adult and consents in writing;
- but a contrary intention to the last three points can be shown in the trust instrument;
- it is assumed a provision for accumulation preclude the possibility of advancement.

10. Many problems arise from definition of advancement in s32 and were considered in *Pilkington v IRC* (1964) – including:
    - it was immaterial that the minor would not receive the property till much later because advancement is not necessarily about getting the property early but about the beneficiary being set up in life;
    - it does not matter that other people benefit from the advance;
    - it is not a problem that arrangement is by creation of a new trust;
    - necessity to delegate trustee powers was not a problem either;
    - but offending the perpetuity period will invalidate the advance.

11. Trustees in making an advancement must bear in mind the need to supervise the transaction and the use of the advance (*Re Pauling's Settlement Trusts* (1964)).

CHAPTER 12

VARIATION OF TRUSTS

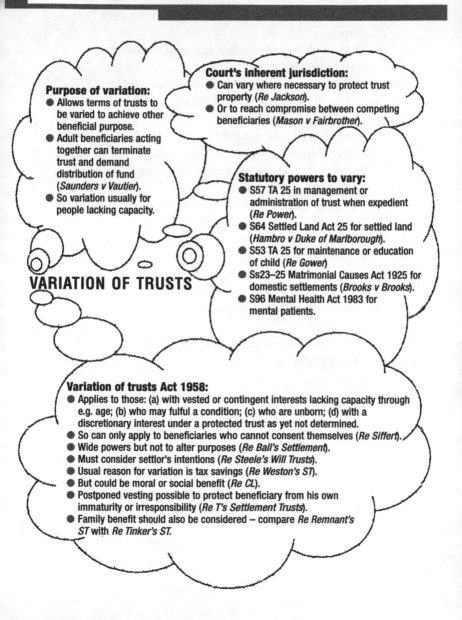

Purpose of variation:
- Allows terms of trusts to be varied to achieve other beneficial purpose.
- Adult beneficiaries acting together can terminate trust and demand distribution of fund (*Saunders v Vautier*).
- So variation usually for people lacking capacity.

Court's inherent jurisdiction:
- Can vary where necessary to protect trust property (*Re Jackson*).
- Or to reach compromise between competing beneficiaries (*Mason v Fairbrother*).

Statutory powers to vary:
- S57 TA 25 in management or administration of trust when expedient (*Re Power*).
- S64 Settled Land Act 25 for settled land (*Hambro v Duke of Marlborough*).
- S53 TA 25 for maintenance or education of child (*Re Gower*)
- Ss23–25 Matrimonial Causes Act 1925 for domestic settlements (*Brooks v Brooks*).
- S96 Mental Health Act 1983 for mental patients.

VARIATION OF TRUSTS

Variation of trusts Act 1958:
- Applies to those: (a) with vested or contingent interests lacking capacity through e.g. age; (b) who may fulful a condition; (c) who are unborn; (d) with a discretionary interest under a protected trust as yet not determined.
- So can only apply to beneficiaries who cannot consent themselves (*Re Siffert*).
- Wide powers but not to alter purposes (*Re Ball's Settlement*).
- Must consider settlor's intentions (*Re Steele's Will Trusts*).
- Usual reason for variation is tax savings (*Re Weston's ST*).
- But could be moral or social benefit (*Re CL*).
- Postponed vesting possible to protect beneficiary from his own immaturity or irresponsibility (*Re T's Settlement Trusts*).
- Family benefit should also be considered – compare *Re Remnant's ST* with *Re Tinker's ST*.

12.1 THE NEED FOR VARIATION

1. The basic concept of variation is simple – to allow the terms of the trust to be altered to achieve some beneficial purpose.
2. Trustees alone cannot alter the trust – this would be a breach of trust.
3. An adult beneficiary who is *sui juris* would be able to deal with his/her own beneficial interest as (s)he saw fit.
4. Similarly, all the beneficiaries, if adult and absolutely entitled, may act together to terminate the trust and demand distribution of fund (*Saunders v Vautier* (1841)).
5. People lacking capacity, e.g. children, cannot deal with their interest in this way.
6. Variation is often, but not always, for tax saving.
7. The courts can use various devices to vary the trust:
   - by using their inherent jurisdiction;
   - by certain specific statutory provisions;
   - by application of Variation of Trusts Act 1958 – but only for certain beneficiaries who could not consent to variation themselves.

12.2 VARIATION UNDER THE INHERENT JURISDICTION OF THE COURTS

1. The court can use inherent jurisdiction to vary a trust where it is absolutely necessary in an emergency to protect the trust, i.e. to use fund to prevent collapse of a building owned by trust (*Re Jackson* (1882)).
2. It can also use inherent jurisdiction to reach a compromise in a dispute between beneficiaries (*Mason v Farbrother* (1983)).
3. Providing that the dispute is genuine (*Chapman v Chapman* (1954)).

12.3 VARIATION UNDER STATUTORY PROVISIONS

1. By s57(1) Trustee Act 1925 court may grant variation 'Where in the management or administration of any property vested in trustees, any sale, lease, mortgage, surrender, release, or other disposition, or any purchase, investment, acquisition, expenditure or other transaction, is in the opinion of the court expedient, but the same cannot be effected by reason of the absence of any power for that purpose vested in the trustees by the trust instrument, if any, or by law, the court may by order confer upon the trustees ... the necessary power ...'

   - so 'expedient' is significantly broader than 'emergency' which is used in the inherent jurisdiction;
   - but the power is only available for 'management or administration';
   - so s57 has been used, e.g. – to buy a house for tenant for life to live in *Re Power* (1947), and to widen a charity's investment powers to make it more efficient (*Re Shipwrecked Fishermen and Mariners' Royal Benevolent Society* (1959)).

2. Variation is also possible under s64(1) Settled Land Act 1925 where it is 'for the benefit of the settled land ... or the person interested under the settlement' if change is one that 'could have validly been effected by an absolute owner' (*Hambro v Duke of Marlborough* (1994)).

3. By s53 TA 1925 the court can authorise various dealings with property held on trust for a child for 'the maintenance, education, or benefit' of the child – though this is an overlap with s57 it can be used, e.g. to bar entails (*Re Gower's Settlement* (1934)).

4. Ss23–25 Matrimonial Causes Act 1973 give the court wide powers to make orders in matrimonial proceedings in respect of both spouses and children (*Brooks v Brooks* (1996)).

5. By s96(1)(d) Mental Health Act 1983 the Court of Protection may vary a settlement in favour of a mental patient.

12.4 VARIATION UNDER THE VARIATION OF TRUSTS ACT 1958

1. Contains the widest powers for the courts to allow variation of trusts.
2. However, the Act only applies to a restrictive range of people – basis of the courts' power being to consent to variations on behalf of people who could not consent for themselves – so s1 includes:

    'Where property, whether real or personal, is held on trusts arising under any will, settlement, or other disposition, the court may, if it thinks fit, by order approve ... any arrangement (by whomsoever proposed) varying or revoking all or any of the trusts, or enlarging the powers of the trustees. The court has the power to give approval on behalf of the following categories:

    (a) any person having, directly or indirectly, an interest, whether vested or contingent, under the trusts, who by reason of infancy or other incapacity is incapable of assenting;

    (b) any person (whether ascertained or not) who may become entitled in future – on a future date, fulfilling a condition, happening of a future event, prospective member of a class;

    (c) any person unborn;

    (d) any person who has a discretionary interest under a protective trust and the interest of the principal beneficiary has not failed or determined.'

3. So the courts will not use 1958 Act in respect of beneficiaries who could consent to the variation themselves (*Re Siffert* (1961)).

4. In applications under the Act all parties should be represented – in the case of those who cannot be represented such as the unborn their interests at least should be represented.

5. While court has wide powers to vary trust, it will not agree to variation that alters original purposes of trust (*Re Ball's Settlement (1969)*

6. And the court will of course in ordering a variation keep in mind the settlor's intentions (*Re Steele's Will Trusts* (1960)).

7. In approving a variation the court must also consider whether or not it will benefit those people for whom it gives its approval if they fall under (a), (b) or (c) of s1 – and 'benefit' can be interpreted in different ways:

   - financial benefit:
     - the classic example of which is tax saving (*Re Weston's Settlements* (1969));
     - which could be avoiding inheritance tax or estate duty (*Re Druce's Settlement Trusts* (1962));
     - or income tax (*Re Clitheroe's Settlement Trusts* (1959)).

   - moral and social benefit:
     - the court should consider the wider benefit and general welfare on whose behalf it is asked to approve a variation (*Re Weston's Settlements* (1969)).
     - and *Weston* shows that the court may be reluctant to allow a variation that will take the trust into a foreign jurisdiction if it is felt not to be a permanent move;
     - though there is contradictory case law (*Re Seal's Marriage Settlement* (1961); *Re Windeatt's Will Trusts* (1969); *Re Whitehead's Will Trusts* (1971));
     - and social benefit might involve doing something for another person that the beneficiary would want if in a position to make the decision (*Re CL* (1969)).

- postponed vesting:
  - the courts will happily delay the date at which an interest vests if this will benefit the beneficiary (*Re Holt's Settlement* (1969));
  - and this may be to protect the beneficiary against their own irresponsibility or immaturity (*Re T's Settlement Trusts* (1961)).
- family benefit:
  - the court may consider whether the existing trust may damage family relations (*Re Remnant's Settlement Trusts* (1970));
  - but may also take a narrower view of family benefits to focus on financial benefits (*Re Tinker's Settlement Trusts* (1960)).

CHAPTER 13

BREACH OF TRUST AND REMEDIES

Personal liability:
- Beneficiary entitled to have trust administered according to provisions of trust (*Target Holdings v Redfern*).
- Trustee is liable to account for all profits made from trust position and any losses caused to trust (*Re Miller's*).
- By s30 TA 25 trustee not liable unless in wilful default (*Armitage v Nurse*).
- Beneficiary cannot sue if participates in breach (*Re Pauling's*) – and s61 TA 25 protects trustee who acts honestly and reasonably.
- Trust instrument may exempt trustee from liability.
- Breach of trust action must be within 6 years (s21 Limitation Act 1980).

Tracing:
- Common law tracing possible if funds unmixed and till identifiable (*Taylor v Plumer*).
- Even if transferred to third party (*Banque Belgique v Hambrook*).
- Three basic conditions for tracing to apply in equity.
  - claim must be founded on an initial fiduciary relationship;
  - property is in a traceable form;
  - must be equitable to trace.
- Unmixed funds or property used to buy other things then can still trace (*Re Hallet's Estate*).
- If in mixed funds can still trace if still identifiable (*Re Tilley's Will Trust*).
- Unless reduced below level of trust.
- If property transferred to third party – then cannot trace against bona fide purchaser – volunteer is bound by trust.

BREACH AND REMEDIES

Injunctions:
- Usually only enforceable if prohibitory.
- Perpetual – settle claim: interim – for where claimant would suffer if forced to wait for full claim – *quia timet* – no loss but used to prevent infringements.
- Granted subject to 'balance of convenience' test from *American Cyanamid v Ethicon*.
- Can grant perpetual injunction but suspend operation so defendant can comply (*Pride of Derby Angling Association v British Celanese*).
- Not granted if claimant delays or acquiesces, order will harm defendant or claimant behaves inequitably.
- By s50 Supreme Court Act 1980 can give damages in lieu if: injury to claimant small, or capable of assessment in monetary terms, or oppressive to grant injunction (*Shelfer v City of London Electric Lighting Co.*).

Other equitable remedies:
Specific performance:
- Only if: Contract already exists; requirement yet to be performed; damages inadequate; property is unique; order can be overseen by the courts.
- Not possible if: would cause hardship; claimant's conduct unconscionable, delay property misdescribed; policy dictates.

Rescission
- Possible for mistake, undue influence, misrepresentation.
- But lost if *restitutio in integrum* not possible, delay, affirmation.

Rectification:
- To correct inaccurate document.

13.1 BREACH OF TRUST AND LIABILITY

1. Lord Browne-Wilkinson in *Target Holdings Ltd v Redferns* (1996): 'Basic right of ... beneficiary is to have ... trust duly administered in accordance with ... provisions of ... trust, if any, and ... general law.'
2. So if trustee fails in duty he is personally liable for loss even if acted in belief that what he did was in best interests of trust (*Re Brogden* (1888)).
3. Trustee must account for any profit made from trust and make good any loss (*Nant-y-glo and Blaina Ironworks Co. v Grave* (1878)).
4. Beneficiary must show both breach of trust and loss caused by the breach (*Re Miller's Trust Deed* (1978)).
5. In *Target Holdings Ltd v Redferns* (1996) Lord Browne-Wilkinson said damages should be measured at date of judgment not breach (so not like common law damages) – loss here was after breach.

13.2 PERSONAL REMEDIES AND PROPRIETARY REMEDIES

13.2.1 The personal remedy against trustees

1. The trustee is personally liable to beneficiaries for incidental profit gained from a breach of trust or loss caused to the trust.
2. S30 TA 1925: 'trustee shall not unless guilty of wilful default be liable for the acts and defaults of other trustees' – so liable for own breaches:
   - in *Re Vickery* (1931) wilful default was described as consciousness or recklessness by the trustee;
   - in *Armitage v Nurse* (1998) it was reaffirmed as when trustee 'consciously takes a risk that loss will result or is recklessly indifferent as to whether it will or not'.

3. Liability may also arise where a trustee does nothing about a breach of trust by other trustees of which he is aware.
4. An incoming trustee is generally not liable for past breaches – but has a duty to take action, even legal action, against a trustee in breach.
5. A retired trustee is only liable for the breaches of other trustees if he retired in order to make the breach possible (*Head v Gould* (1898)).
6. Trustees are jointly and severally liable if all responsible for breach or those in breach are assisted by wilful default of others – but by Civil Liability (Contribution) Act 1981 court can decide what is fair for each.
7. One trustee may be obliged to indemnify another, e.g. solicitor trustee exercising control over lay trustee (*Chillingworth v Chambers* (1896)) – or trustee is fraudulent in procuring breach (*Bahin v Hughes* (1886)).
8. Personal liability is set against profit made by trustee or loss suffered by trust (*Target Holdings Ltd v Redferns* (1996)).

13.2.2 Defences to an action for personal liability

1. A beneficiary who participates in a breach of trust cannot sue on the breach (*Re Paulings Settlement Trust* (1964)):
   * beneficiary must have been aware of the breach;
   * and must have freely agreed to it with no undue influence;
   * and must have fully understood what he was agreeing to;
   * there is no need to show beneficiary gained from breach.
2. Where the beneficiary acquiesces or releases the trustee from liability this has same effect as if beneficiary agreed to breach from start.
3. S62 TA 1925 allows court to impound the interests of a beneficiary who has instigated or consented to a breach of trust.

4. S61 TA 1925 allows court discretion to relieve a trustee of liability:
   - where the trustee acted honestly and reasonably; and
   - where it would be fair to excuse him from liability;
   - trustee must show he has acted prudently – what relieves trustee from liability is a question of fact in each case (*Re Turner* (1897)).

13.2.3 Excluding liability

1. Sometimes the trust instrument expressly states that the trustee is not liable for acts or omissions that would otherwise be a breach of trust.
2. This may then give the trustee a good defence to a claim of breach of trust by the beneficiaries (*Armitage v Nurse* (1997)).

13.2.4 Limitation

1. By s21(3) Limitation Act 1980 'action by a beneficiary to recover trust property or in respect of any breach' must be brought within six years.
2. There are certain exceptions:
   - where the beneficiary's interest is in the future;
   - where the beneficiary lacked capacity to bring the action earlier;
   - where the action by the beneficiary involves fraud by the trustee;
   - where the action involves trust property converted to trustee's use.

13.2.5 Tracing as a proprietary remedy

1. Applies where, e.g. a trustee has insufficient funds to make good a loss arising from a breach of trust, or intermingled the fund with his own.

2. So it involves tracing the trust property into its changed form.

3. Because remedy is *in rem* rather than *in personam*, right to trace is not lost merely because of trustee's insolvency – the right taking priority over unsecured creditors.

13.2.6 Tracing in common law

1. At common law a beneficiary may trace trust property as long as it is still identifiable and unmixed with other funds (*Taylor v Plumer* (1815)) – and common law tracing applies to chattels particularly.

2. And this applies even where the property has been transferred to a third party (*Banque Belge v Hambrook* (1921)).

3. And where trustee has invested property at a profit, tracing extends to profit as well as original property (*Trustees of the Property of FC Jones v Jones* (1997)).

4. But unlike in equity, common law tracing not allowed where trust property has become mixed.

13.2.7 Tracing in equity

1. Usually by beneficiaries against trustees because in common law beneficiaries have no interest in trust property as against the trustees.

2. Three basic conditions for tracing to apply in equity:
   - claim must be founded on an initial fiduciary relationship;
   - there must be property in a traceable form;
   - it must be equitable to trace.

3. What is a 'fiduciary relationship' has been widely drawn by courts, eg:
   - executors of a will and residual beneficiaries (*Re Diplock* (1948));

- a bank receiving money from another bank under a mistake of fact (*Chase Manhattan Bank v Israel–British Bank* (1981)).

4. Unless property is in a 'traceable form' remedy is unavailable because 'equity does nothing in vain – see *Re Diplock* (1948).

5. If the fund remains unmixed the claimant can trace it:
   - and if it has been sold then the claimant may take the proceeds;
   - and if proceeds are used to buy other property can take that or use it as security for amount of trust fund (*Re Hallett's Estate* (1880)).

6. If fund has become mixed, still can trace if property remains identifiable:
   - 'If a trustee amalgamated trust property with his own, the beneficiary will be entitled to every portion of the property which the trustee cannot prove to be his own': Ungoed-Thomas J in *Re Tilley's Will Trust* (1967);
   - so if the mixed fund is reduced below the amount of the trust fund then that part of the trust fund must have been spent;
   - later payments in are not treated as repayments by trustee – so to trace must ascertain what is the 'lowest intermediate balance';
   - if trustee becomes bankrupt after wrongly mixing trust funds with own funds tracing beneficiaries can trace to gain priority over other creditors – but if funds lawfully mixed then cannot (*Space Investments Ltd v Canadian Imperial Bank of Commerce Trust Co (Bahamas) Ltd* (1986)).

7. Where trustee in breach of trust has transferred property to third party whether tracing can apply depends on who third party is:
   - cannot trace against bona fide purchaser for value without notice;

- if third party is an innocent volunteer then tracing possible because (s)he takes subject to trust, provided beneficiary shows a proprietary interest and property is in traceable form;
- But if full restitution inequitable doctrine of 'change of position' may provide defence to tracing (*Lipkin Gorman v Karpnale Ltd* (1991)).

13.3 EQUITABLE REMEDIES – INJUNCTIONS

13.3.1 Introduction

1. As an equitable remedy, injunctions:
   - arise from the power to act *in personam*;
   - can result in contempt of court if not complied with;
   - are at the discretion of the court.
2. They may be perpetual, interim or ancillary.
3. Granted by High Court by s37(1) Supreme Court Act 1981 'in all cases in which it appears just and convenient to do so'.
4. County Court – has similar powers but cannot issue search orders or freezing injunctions.
5. In *Carolina Insurance v Assurantie* Lord Brandon identified where to grant injunction: (i) where one party has invaded or intends to invade an enforceable legal or equitable right; (ii) where behaviour of party against whom injunction is sought is unconscionable.

13.3.2 Types of injunctions

1. Prohibitory injunctions must be distinguished from mandatory:
   - **prohibitory** – prevent breach of a legal or equitable right;

- **mandatory** – rarely granted as impose positive obligations and hard to enforce – but prohibitory with positive effect have been granted *Sky Petroleum Ltd v VIP Petroleum Ltd* (1974)

2. Perpetual injunctions (final relief) should be distinguished from interim (interlocutory – before Woolf reforms):
   - **perpetual** would settle the dispute – so only granted where damages is an inadequate remedy;
   - **interim** are granted where claimant might suffer irreparable harm if forced to wait for main action.
3. *Quia timet* injunctions – granted when no harm has yet been caused but claimant is trying to prevent future infringements of his rights:
   - can be both prohibitory and mandatory;
   - and perpetual or interim;
   - claimant must show very strong probability of future infringement of rights – Lord Upjohn in *Redland Bricks Ltd v Morris* (1970).

13.3.3 General rules in granting injunctions

1. Discretionary remedy – so only awarded where damages inadequate.
2. It is argued whether or not public interest should be considered – compare *Miller v Jackson* (1977) and *Kennaway v Thompson* (1981).
3. Failure to comply is contempt of court.
4. Will not usually be granted against the Crown (Crown Proceedings Act 1947) – but see *Factortame* (1990).

13.3.4 Perpetual injunctions

1. Not granted if damages is an adequate remedy.
2. With mandatory injunctions enforcement is the main problem:
   - two types: (i) remedy to restore claimant to position prior to damage – and prohibitory could have been

granted if sought before wrongful act; (ii) order is for defendant to carry out a positive act;
- not granted if involve performing continuing positive obligations (*Gravesham Borough Council v British Railways Board* (1978));
- extent of damage – and possible harm to defendant may be considered (*Wrotham Park Estate v Parkside Homes Ltd* (1974)).

3. Can grant injunction but suspend operation so defendant can comply with terms (*Pride of Derby Angling Association v British Celanese and Others* (1953)).

13.3.5 Interim injunctions

1. Can be prohibitory, mandatory or *quia timet.*
2. Granted subject to rule that nothing should be done that may prejudice final outcome at trial or permanently damage position of either party.
3. Formerly based on showing – strong *prima facie* case of infringement of rights, damages inadequate, balance of convenience favoured grant.
4. Rules generally now in Lord Diplock's test in *American Cyanamid Co v Ethicon Ltd* (1975):
   - court is satisfied claim is neither frivolous or vexatious; and
   - court is satisfied that there is a serious issue to try; and
   - so test of whether injunction is granted is based on balance of convenience test;
   - as last resort only – court may consider relative strength of each party's case.
5. Although Lord Denning preferred previous *prima facie* case approach (*Fellowes v Fisher (1975)* and *Hubbard v Pitt* (1976)).
6. Generally, courts use balance of convenience test with no reference to merits of either party's case (*Series 5 Software v Clarke* (1996)).

13.3.6 Defences to claims for injunctions

1. Delay in seeking order by claimant:
   - so will not be granted if delay is unreasonable;
   - an acceptable delay is less for interim than for permanent relief;
   - but grant also depends on facts – compare *Shepherd Homes v Sandham* (1971) with *Kelsen v Imperial Tobacco Co Ltd* (1957).
2. Acquiescence:
   - the inference is that claimant has accepted interference with his rights (*Sayers v Collyer* (1885));
   - modern approach: (i) was defendant encouraged to believe he was entitled to act as he did?; (ii) if so, did this cause him detriment?; (iii) if so was it unconscionable for claimant then to assert his right?
3. Hardship to defendant:
   - can be taken into account, particularly with mandatory injunctions;
   - hardship can be avoided by granting injunction but suspending it.
4. Conduct of claimant:
   - all equitable maxims apply as remedy is discretionary;
   - so, e.g. claimant must come to court with clean hands.

13.3.7 Damages in lieu of injunctions

1. Now under s50 Supreme Court Act 1981 – court can award damages where none are available in law. e.g. *quia timet*.
2. So main requirement is that court has jurisdiction to grant injunctions.
3. Damages awarded according to conditions in *Shelfer v City of London Electric Lighting Co* (1895):
   - injury to claimant is only small;
   - injury is capable of assessment in monetary terms;

- injury would be adequately compensated by a small payment;
- case is one where it would be oppressive to grant an injunction.

13.4 EQUITABLE REMEDIES – SPECIFIC PERFORMANCE

13.4.1 General principles

1. Equitable order of court that defendant should carry out terms of a contractual agreement.
2. Granted at the discretion of court – so it is only allowed where:
   - contract already exists – because equity will not assist a volunteer;
   - some requirement in contract is yet to be performed;
   - damages inadequate – damages normally considered appropriate remedy so must be special circumstances;
   - the property under the agreement is unique;
   - the order can be overseen by the courts – compare *Ryan v Mutual Tontine (Westminster Chambers) Association* (1893) with *Posner v Scott-Lewis* (1987);
   - person seeking order must comply with equitable maxims and have performed or be ready to perform his side of the bargain;
   - must not cause hardship to other party (*Spiller v Bolton* (1947)).
3. One significant restriction is order will not be granted without mutuality
   - i.e. it will not be granted against one party unless it could also be awarded against the other (*Price v Strange* (1977)).
   - so this rule will be applied, e.g. where the party seeking the order lacks capacity (*Flight v Bolland* (1828)).

13.4.2 Defences

1. The court may exercise discretion to refuse specific performance.
2. It may do so where:
   - order would cause real hardship (*Patel v Ali* (1984)) or injustice as in mistake or misrepresentation (*Webster v Cecil* (1861));
   - where claimant's conduct is inequitable (*Quadrant Visual Communications Ltd v Hutchinson Telephone (UK) Ltd* (1991));
   - in the case of laches or unreasonable delay (*Mills v Haywood* (1877)) – although there is no statutory limitation period to bar a claim, time is generally not of the essence in equity, and there is no hard and fast definition of what is an unreasonable delay;
   - property is misdescribed;
   - public policy dictates.

13.5 EQUITABLE REMEDIES – RESCISSION

1. Rescission is possible where an agreement is based on:
   - a mistake not void by common law (*Solle v Butcher* (1950));
   - a misrepresentation (*Heilbut Symons & Co v Buckleton* (1913));
   - undue influence (*Barclays Bank v O'Brien* (1993)).
2. But bars to rescission include:
   - that *restitutio in integrum* is impossible (*Cheese v Thomas* (1994));
   - laches or unreasonable delay (*Allcard v Skinner* (1887));
   - acquisition of rights by innocent third party (*Re Eastgate* (1905));
   - affirmation, e.g. by taking benefits (*Peyman v Lanjani* (1985)).

13.6 EQUITABLE REMEDIES – RECTIFICATION

1. This is an order of the court to correct an inaccurate document.
2. So it applies where 'the parties were in complete agreement on the terms of their contract, but by an error wrote them down wrongly': Lord Denning in *Frederick E Rose Ltd v William Pim Jnr & Co* (1953).
3. So party seeking order needs convincing proof that document does not represent each party's intentions (*Jocelyne v Nissen* (1970)).

INDEX